TEEN BOY'S SURVIVAL GUIDE

From Making Friends, Building Confidence, Overcoming Challenges, Preparing for the Future, and Everything in Between

JAMIE MYERS

ISBN: 978-1-957590-37-0

For questions, email: Support@AwesomeReads.org

Please consider writing a review!

Just visit: AwesomeReads.org/review

Copyright 2024. All Rights Reserved.

No part of this book may be reproduced or transmitted in any form or by any means, electronic or mechanical, including photocopying, recording, or by any other form without written permission from the publisher.

FREE BONUS

SCAN TO GET OUR NEXT BOOK FOR FREE!

TABLE OF CONTENTS

INTRODUCTION: THE JOURNEY OF ADOLESCENCE 1

CHAPTER ONE: UNDERSTANDING PUBERTY AND PHYSICAL CHANGES 5

    THE SCIENCE OF PUBERTY 6

    DEALING WITH GROWTH SPURTS 8

    UNDERSTANDING BODILY CHANGES 10

    MENTAL CHANGES DURING PUBERTY 12

CHAPTER TWO: BUILDING CONFIDENCE AND SELF-ESTEEM 17

    DEFINING CONFIDENCE AND SELF-ESTEEM 18

    UNDERSTANDING THE IMPORTANCE OF SELF-WORTH 20

    HOW TO BUILD YOUR CONFIDENCE, SELF-ESTEEM, AND SELF-WORTH 21

    OVERCOMING SELF-DOUBT 24

CHAPTER THREE: IMPORTANT LIFE SKILLS 27

    BASIC COOKING SKILLS 28

    MONEY MANAGEMENT AND BUDGETING 34

    TIME MANAGEMENT AND ORGANIZATION 36

    COMMUNICATION AND SOCIAL SKILLS 39

CHAPTER FOUR: NAVIGATING FRIENDSHIPS 41

    MAKING NEW FRIENDS 42

    MAINTAINING LONG-TERM FRIENDSHIPS 43

    DEALING WITH CONFLICT IN FRIENDSHIPS 44

UNDERSTANDING THE VALUE OF FRIENDSHIP 45
CHAPTER FIVE: UNDERSTANDING PEER PRESSURE 47
    RECOGNIZING PEER PRESSURE 48
    STRATEGIES TO RESIST PEER PRESSURE 49
    THE ROLE OF ASSERTIVENESS 50
    LEARNING FROM PEER PRESSURE EXPERIENCES 52
CHAPTER SIX: PHYSICAL HEALTH AND FITNESS 55
    IMPORTANCE OF EXERCISE AND FITNESS 56
    HEALTHY EATING HABITS 57
    SLEEP AND REST: ESSENTIAL ELEMENTS OF HEALTH 61
    PREVENTING COMMON SPORTS INJURIES 64
CHAPTER SEVEN: MENTAL HEALTH AWARENESS 69
    UNDERSTANDING STRESS AND ANXIETY 70
    WAYS TO MANAGE STRESS 70
    THE IMPORTANCE OF EMOTIONAL WELL-BEING 72
    IDENTIFYING SIGNS OF DEPRESSION 73
    WHEN AND HOW TO SEEK HELP 75
CHAPTER EIGHT: UNDERSTANDING AND EXPRESSING EMOTIONS 77
    RECOGNIZING DIFFERENT EMOTIONS 78
    HEALTHY WAYS TO EXPRESS FEELINGS 82
    COPING WITH UNCOMFORTABLE EMOTIONS 84
    EMOTIONAL REGULATION SKILLS 86

CHAPTER NINE: BALANCING SCHOOL AND EXTRACURRICULAR ACTIVITIES 89

TIME MANAGEMENT STRATEGIES 90
FINDING THE RIGHT EXTRACURRICULAR ACTIVITIES 91
SETTING BOUNDARIES AND PRIORITIES 95
AVOIDING BURNOUT 97

CHAPTER TEN: ACADEMIC SUCCESS AND PREPARING FOR THE FUTURE 99

SETTING PERSONAL AND ACADEMIC GOALS 100
STUDY SKILLS AND LEARNING STRATEGIES 101
PREPARING FOR COLLEGE AND CAREER PATHS 101
EXPLORING INTERESTS AND PASSIONS 103

CHAPTER ELEVEN: SOCIAL MEDIA AND ONLINE SAFETY 107

UNDERSTANDING DIGITAL CITIZENSHIP 108
PRIVACY AND SECURITY ONLINE 109
THE IMPACT OF SOCIAL MEDIA ON MENTAL HEALTH 112
DEALING WITH CYBERBULLYING 114

CHAPTER TWELVE: LEARNING RESPONSIBILITY AND INDEPENDENCE 117

BECOMING SELF-RELIANT 118
DEVELOPING RESPONSIBILITY AND ACCOUNTABILITY 119
UNDERSTANDING THE IMPORTANCE OF HARD WORK 120
PREPARING FOR ADULTHOOD 121

CHAPTER THIRTEEN: RESPECTING DIVERSITY AND INCLUSION 123
- UNDERSTANDING DIFFERENT CULTURES AND BACKGROUNDS 124
- RECOGNIZING AND COMBATING STEREOTYPES AND PREJUDICES 125
- THE IMPORTANCE OF EMPATHY AND UNDERSTANDING 127
- ADVOCATING FOR EQUALITY 127

CHAPTER FOURTEEN: OVERCOMING CHALLENGES AND BUILDING RESILIENCE 129
- UNDERSTANDING FAILURE AND SETBACKS 130
- STRATEGIES FOR BUILDING RESILIENCE 132
- THE ROLE OF A POSITIVE MINDSET 133
- LEARNING FROM MISTAKES AND EXPERIENCES 134

CONCLUSION: STEPPING INTO ADULTHOOD 135

INTRODUCTION: THE JOURNEY OF ADOLESCENCE

If you are reading this book, you're probably getting ready to jump into the exciting time of your life, where you leave childhood behind and start to become an adult. This is the time you learn how to be your own person and decide who you want to be. It can be a wild ride with a lot of ups and downs, good and bad, but most importantly, plenty of personal growth.

Adolescence is an important time in your life that will shape what kind of man you'll become. It's the perfect time to discover your strengths, build your confidence, and learn essential skills that can enable you to navigate your life now and later as an adult.

This book was written with you in mind. Throughout these pages, you'll learn how you can understand some of the challenges you'll be facing at this unique time of life and the best ways to overcome them. You don't have to figure out all these adventures alone.

You'll get the chance to learn about a wide variety of topics that you will face during these teen years, from understanding puberty to building yourself up to handling different social and academic situations.

This book also imparts some great information about basic life skills, like cooking, money management, and communication. Having these skills will prepare you to lead a successful, happy, and healthy life.

Facing peer pressure and conflict might also be part of your teenage experience, so this book discusses ways to resist and handle these forces like a champ. That way, you can be your best and happiest self, prioritizing friendships and relationships that support you instead of holding you back.

Taking care of your health, both mentally and physically, is a top priority during this time. To that end, you'll learn about the importance of exercise, eating right, and getting enough sleep. It's also important that you are aware of some of the mental health issues you might face, like anxiety and depression.

Given all of the new and exciting (or sometimes not exciting) things that are going to be happening to you, we'll look together at the unique emotional roller coaster you'll soon be riding. With this book, you'll know what to expect and how to start developing important coping skills.

Balancing school and extracurriculars is also going to become a challenge. Both are so important—that's why we will take the time to strategize ways of staying on top of these two key areas of life. School is important for opening doors in the future, but it's also important for figuring out what you like to do and the kind of person you want to be.

Now that you are growing older, you'll learn about personal responsibility and how you should handle being a digital citizen, respecting diversity, and living independently. And maybe, most importantly, you'll learn about how to be a resilient person.

Teen Boy's Survival Guide covers sensitive topics, tough issues, and all the other nitty-gritty concerns that come with being a teenager.

Take the time to read this book and mark places that you feel might apply to you. Then, go back and read again to learn as much as possible. The more you learn, the better equipped you'll be to handle being a teenager and become a positive force in the world.

CHAPTER ONE:
UNDERSTANDING PUBERTY AND PHYSICAL CHANGES

Going from childhood to manhood will bring many changes, with puberty bringing some of the most dramatic ones. There is no set schedule for puberty. It can be confusing and even scary at times, but it's perfectly normal, and the more you know, the more prepared you can be. It's a time of great change but also a time of great opportunity. This will be the time you determine who you want to be.

THE SCIENCE OF PUBERTY

While puberty can seem scary, it doesn't have to be if you know what's causing it and what to expect. It's a process that everyone goes through, and you'll survive it too.

Be prepared; puberty can start as early as the age of twelve and progress until sixteen and beyond. Furthermore, there's no right or wrong time for puberty to start because everyone is different. Even though you might see some of your friends start going through the changes of puberty, it doesn't mean that you are behind — no matter when you start, everyone goes through it eventually. It's a natural process that moves at its own pace.

The hypothalamus, which is a small, pea-sized part of your brain, starts to send gonadotropin-releasing hormones to the pituitary gland. The pituitary gland begins making follicle-stimulating hormones (FSH) and luteinizing hormones (LH).

The pituitary gland and the hypothalamus are both located in your brain.

The LH causes your testicles to grow, which produces a hormone called testosterone. Hormones are the chemical messengers that travel through your bloodstream to tell your body what to do next.

Testosterone is what causes your body to change from a boy into a man. It makes your muscles grow, causes your voice to deepen, and stimulates hair growth in new places. It also causes your mood to change. In fact, you might find that you're more easily angered or that you have mood swings when this hormone comes to call.

FSH also causes your testes to start producing testosterone and control the amount of sperm your body is producing. Sperm is what allows men to conceive children.

If you have questions about any of the changes your body is experiencing or what you are going through, it's important to talk to a trusted adult. They can help you understand what's happening and provide support. Remember, puberty is a temporary phase, and it will eventually pass. In the meantime, try to enjoy the journey and focus on the positive changes that are happening to you.

While going through puberty, you'll experience five stages.

Stage 1: Your body is starting to change, and hormones are getting active. There aren't any outside signs of what's going on yet, but your body is busy, nonetheless. The LH and FSH hormones are building up in your body.

Stage 2: You'll notice pubic hair is starting to form, and your penis and scrotum are getting larger.

Stage 3: You'll suddenly grow taller, your penis and testicles will get bigger, your muscles will start getting larger, and your voice will start to change and crack.

Stage 4: Your armpits will produce hair, you might have acne that starts to form, and your voice will become permanently deeper.

Stage 5: Your muscles will start to fill out, your maximum height will be reached, and you'll start shaving due to increased facial hair.

Keep in mind that some of these stages might overlap or be different for you; no two people are exactly alike.

DEALING WITH GROWTH SPURTS

One of the exciting changes that happens during puberty is growth spurts, which are caused by growth hormones.

A growth spurt is when you grow more quickly than usual. You can expect to see a huge growth, sometimes two to four inches, in just a year. Lifestyle choices can impact your growth; if you want to maximize the potential of your growth spurt, here are some easy suggestions to follow:

1: Stay Physical

Getting outside to run and bike is an easy way to keep your body healthy. Find activities you enjoy, like getting involved in sports or martial arts at the local YMCA or rec center. Even staying inside and doing muscle-building exercises like squats, push-ups, and planks can help prepare your body for growth spurts. Staying active can help improve your mood, reduce stress, and increase growth spurts and muscle mass. Try to be active for at least sixty minutes a day.

Some exercises to stay healthy:

- Biking
- Running
- Walking
- Football
- Basketball
- Wrestling
- Baseball

- Push-ups
- Squats
- Planks

2: Get Plenty of Sleep

Staying up late and rolling out of bed early in the morning might seem like an easy thing to do, but you aren't doing yourself any favors. Getting enough sleep is a key part of growing to your full potential. All the experts say that getting eight to ten hours of sleep is ideal. The reason why sleep is so important is because your body produces the most growth hormones at night. The more growth hormones your body can produce, the more you grow.

3: Get the Right Vitamins

Making sure to eat foods that have lots of *the right vitamins* is important. Vitamins are the building blocks that allow your body to do its best. All living things need vitamins, even animals and plants. If you don't have enough essential vitamins, it can keep you from growing in height and muscle mass. In fact, if you're wondering what foods you need to eat to get the most important vitamins, look no further:

> **Iron** ensures that your blood cells can carry oxygen to all the different parts of your body. Foods that are rich in iron include spinach, broccoli, lentils, healthy cuts of beef, and fresh nuts or seeds.
>
> **Calcium** keeps your bones growing and staying strong while also helping your teeth stay healthy. Foods that are rich in calcium include yogurt, almonds, leafy greens, and even tofu.
>
> **Vitamin D** also promotes strong bone mass. Foods that are rich in vitamin D include eggs, salmon, and soy milk.

Also, dark chocolate has lots of iron and can be great for you, but only in moderation (the right amount).

UNDERSTANDING BODILY CHANGES

Your body will go through many physical changes from the time you start puberty until you reach maturity. While all of these changes are normal and to be expected, you should remember that no two people have the same experience while going through puberty. Be patient, and your body will move at the speed that's best for you.

Physical Changes

Growth Spurt: You can expect to grow several inches, sometimes two to four inches a year, during puberty. This usually happens during the first couple of years, which can start around twelve to fourteen, but which might be earlier or later depending on what your body feels is right.

Weight Gain: Not only will you be growing taller, but you will probably start to gain weight. This weight gain comes from the increase in the mass of your muscles and the density of your bones. This is a great time to start working out and building up your muscles.

Changes in Body Shape: Expect to see your shoulders broaden and all your muscles start to grow. You'll likely become more muscular and slimmer if you stick to a healthy diet and lifestyle. Some exceptions and variations in body shape occur when you are genetically predisposed toward a certain physique, have an underlying physical or mental health condition, or are otherwise unique. No matter what changes you encounter during this time, the most important thing is that you take care of your body and feel comfortable in it.

Hair Growth on Your Face: Most young men experience hair growth with puberty. If you belong to this group, the first hair you'll see will be on your upper lip. Then, your cheeks will start to produce hair. The hairs start growing scarcely but will become thicker and darker over time. This thick, dark hair is called vellus hair, making up beards, mustaches, and sideburns.

Underarm Hair Growth: Along with facial hair growth, you will start to have hair under your arms in your armpits. This is the time to make sure you are wearing deodorant if you haven't been already. Armpit hair can be light, dark, thick, or thin.

Genital Changes: During this time, you'll see some changes in your penis and testicles. Your penis will get bigger and longer as you go through puberty, and your testicles will also grow larger. As you go through these changes, expect to start having unexpected erections and hair growth as well.

Voice Changes: One of the more noticeable changes you'll go through will be your voice changing. At the end of puberty, you can expect your voice to be deeper than before, but until it's done changing, you might experience cracking. Don't worry, as it doesn't last for long. These voice changes are caused by growth in the larynx, also called the voice box.

Acne: Acne occurs when pores are clogged and break out into pimples or zits. This process happens during puberty because of an overproduction of sebum, which is an oily substance that helps keep the skin moist. Knowing how to take care of your skin will help reduce acne — which we'll talk more about later.

You will go through many changes during your teenage years. Some will be great, and some will be less great, but it will all be worth it in the end.

MENTAL CHANGES DURING PUBERTY

You will go through many different changes, and you should also expect to experience emotional and behavioral changes during this time as well.

Emotional Changes During Puberty:

You can expect a lot of emotional changes during puberty; here are some to be aware of:

Mood swings are common. One minute, you might feel happy, and the next, angry or sad. While it can be overwhelming, it is normal to have these extreme feelings; it's part of your body adapting to the new hormones racing through your body, as well as the emotional adjustment to the social and cultural pressures of growing up. Just try not to let them get the best of you.

You might feel more irritable with your family and friends, but it's all part of the process. What's not okay is acting out and being mean to your friends or family when you get overwhelmed by your feelings. If you find yourself running out of patience, try to remember that they care about you and don't want to upset you.

Feelings of anger might sometimes creep up on you, but do your best to take a step back from these feelings. Be patient with yourself and others—this can be a trying experience, but counting to ten and taking deep breaths can help.

Increased sensitivity might also ambush you at unexpected times, making you feel hurt or emotional over something that might not have bothered you before. When you find yourself feeling like crying or attacked by family, remember that you have a lot going on, and this is part of it.

Stress can be another thing that feels a lot bigger than it has in the past. With all your other emotions running full force, small things that might not have worried you much before can now feel overwhelming.

If any of your feelings are too much to deal with, talk with your parents. They will understand and help you manage these feelings so that they won't overwhelm you. Even connecting with friends going through the same thing can help you feel less alone—maybe your friends will even have advice they can share with you for dealing with tricky emotions.

Changes in Behavior During Puberty:

You will also see some changes in your behavior that are completely unlike anything you would have done before. It can be completely overwhelming, but remember, there are people you can talk to who have been through it before.

> **You might find yourself taking bigger risks** than before because you have increased risk-taking behaviors. You might find yourself riding your bike faster or jumping off dangerous places into the pool. Stop and think about whether the pain and hurt that come from these dangers are worth it. If thrill-seeking is your thing, you can always opt for safer alternatives, like catching a horror movie or participating in activities supervised by adult professionals. At the very least, be sure to take precautions, like wearing a helmet, to minimize any danger you're exposing yourself to with more adventurous activities.
>
> **Social withdrawal**, or a lack of interest in hanging out with your friends and family, is also a common part of puberty. It's normal, and there is nothing wrong with spending time by yourself and using that time to explore interests of your own. These may include reading, listening to music, playing video games, or just hanging outside.

If you also find yourself unable to focus in class or when people are talking to you, it can be part of the puberty process. Difficulty concentrating might be a problem for a few years because so much is already going on in your brain. Don't stress; just take the extra time you need to study and take notes.

Expect your sleep habits to change as well, especially later in puberty. Many young men find themselves staying up later and having a harder time getting up in the morning. This is just another change your body might go through.

With all the growth that you are going through, you will need fuel. You should see an increase in your appetite because you'll need additional nutrition and energy for your body and mind. Eating a good and healthy diet lets your body work at its best.

Cognitive Changes During Puberty:

Increased abstract thinking is something you'll gain during this time. You'll be able to understand more complex concepts and start to have even more opinions and ideas.

Improved problem-solving skills will come with the development of your brain. This allows you to become more independent and self-reliant.

You will develop enhanced creativity that might lead to an interest in new hobbies and activities. Follow these interests, and don't be afraid to try out new things.

During this time, you will also start to develop a moral code. It will be a time for you to explore what's right and wrong and decide what values are important to you.

Emotional, behavioral, and cognitive changes during puberty are a normal part of development. If, at any point during your teen years, you feel depressed, sad for an extended time, anxious, or stressed beyond what you think is normal, talk to an adult.

CHAPTER TWO: BUILDING CONFIDENCE AND SELF-ESTEEM

How we think about ourselves affects everything we do. It's important to build confidence and healthy self-esteem during this critical time.

As you get older, you are going to start feeling more independent. This is a good thing, and it's important to learn how to take care of yourself and make your own decisions.

DEFINING CONFIDENCE AND SELF-ESTEEM

What is confidence? Confidence is belief in your abilities. It's a feeling that you can do things well and succeed at what you put your mind to. Confidence also means feeling secure in your authentic self—who you are and not who others expect you to be. Confidence is an important part of success in school, in your personal life, and in pursuing your long-term goals.

It is also important to have confidence so that you feel comfortable trying new things and going after goals. Confidence gives us the strength to continue with something despite it being difficult or challenging. It means that if the goal is worth it, you keep going even when you want to give up. This is also called perseverance, which is often necessary to achieve success.

Confidence also helps us have high self-esteem, which is very important. Self-esteem is a word used to describe how you feel about yourself. It's determined by how much you like and accept yourself—even those parts of yourself that might seem different or vulnerable. If you have low self-esteem, you might feel bad about yourself or feel doubtful even when you shouldn't. Keeping your head high and moving forward is something confidence can help with.

If you often feel negative about your ability to do things and doubt whether you will succeed, you might be suffering from low self-esteem.

Many things can affect a person's self-esteem, but cultivating positive self-esteem is important. Here are some strategies for doing so:

Set Goals: Setting daily and weekly goals is a great way to keep track of all the positive things you have accomplished. Write them down, and every day, spend a few minutes going over the things you have accomplished, no matter how small. Every accomplishment counts.

Positive People: Having friends who support you helps make you feel good about yourself. If your friends are negative or put you down, even jokingly, they are not helping you be your best self. Friends should always build you up and should not try to tear you down.

Positive Self-talk: When you talk about yourself, be sure to be positive and not speak negatively. Being negative about yourself can lead to poor self-esteem over time. Even if you are doing it to be funny, you don't realize how you are affecting yourself and other people's view of you.

Get Help: It's okay to struggle with low self-esteem. If you realize you are having negative feelings about yourself, talk to your parents, a mental health professional, or another trusted adult. They can get you help and build up your self-esteem. Don't ever be ashamed because of your thoughts. The chemicals in your brain, environmental factors, and your unique constitution affect you in ways no one fully understands, and there is nothing wrong with seeking help.

Always believe in yourself because your confidence and self-esteem are some of the most important traits you will develop while going through puberty.

UNDERSTANDING THE IMPORTANCE OF SELF-WORTH

Self-worth is the knowledge that you are valuable and know how important you are. It is also the thing that ensures you know you deserve love, respect, and success. Self-worth allows us to feel good about ourselves and the things we do, and having self-worth allows you to be a positive influence on those around you. Self-worth plays an important role in many aspects of your life:

> **Family:** You can treat your siblings with more patience when you know your self-worth and have more understanding for your parents. Self-worth allows you to have a more positive relationship with your family. It enables you to understand the value that your family offers as well as what you offer to them.
>
> **Friends:** Have you ever had a friend who put people down, maybe in a joking or playful manner? Even if it seems like a joke, putting people down is usually an attempt to make yourself feel better. When you know your self-worth, you don't have to put other people down, and it makes you a better friend.
>
> **School:** It can be hard to meet all the expectations that you have in school, and every year it gets harder. Self-worth will remind you that you deserve good grades. It will be what gives you the motivation to study and put in the effort to get the results worthy of you.
>
> **Sports:** While sports aren't for everybody, if you do find your sport, it's important to try your best. Self-worth helps you strive to be the best you can be and work hard to be the best.
>
> **Hobbies:** Whether you have a hobby you love or if you need the courage to try something new, having high self-worth is what

will let you be brave enough to pursue those hobbies. Some hobbies that you might be interested in could be woodworking, playing an instrument, computer programming, writing, debate, gaming, painting, cooking, collecting, photography, fishing, theater, or biking.

Community: Being involved in your community is another way that self-worth can help you. When you know your self-worth, you want to help other people. It might be through volunteering at your local animal shelter, picking up trash in your neighborhood, or working with young kids trying to learn a sport or a hobby.

Knowing your self-worth allows you to be a positive influence in all aspects of your life while helping others learn their own self-worth.

HOW TO BUILD YOUR CONFIDENCE, SELF-ESTEEM, AND SELF-WORTH

It's easy to say that you need to have all these positive feelings and thoughts, but how do you get there when you aren't feeling so confident right now? Everyone has moments where it's hard to remember how awesome you are, and no one is immune to self-doubt.

Here are some additional tips for increasing your positive self-thoughts:

Set realistic goals and achieve them.

Realistic goals are goals that you can break down into achievable steps within a specific amount of time.

For example, instead of saying, "I want to get better math grades," you might say, "I want to raise my math grade from 85% to 90%."

Not everyone will excel in every category, and that's okay. The world needs people who are good at all kinds of different things. Having an accurate understanding of your strengths and weaknesses will help you set realistic goals.

For example, if your strongest subject isn't math, don't set a goal to get an A+ in calculus. Instead, look at your current grade and set an achievable goal. If football isn't your sport or activity, don't set the goal of becoming a quarterback in three weeks. Allow time to work towards what you want but break it up into smaller goals.

Once you figure out what a realistic goal is, set a deadline. Deadlines help us keep on track with our goals. There is also a component of excitement as deadlines approach, which can help with motivation.

Spend time with positive people.

Surrounding yourself with upbeat and supportive friends can have a huge impact on your quality of life. Positive minded people are more likely to increase your confidence and bring joy into your everyday experiences. Look for people who talk well of you behind your back; are just as generous with their time and resources as you are; and that build you up when they are around.

Ideally, you and your friends will reciprocate the same level of giving and taking with all things. This means that just as much as you invest in them and their wellbeing, they'll also invest back into you. Although relationships should be balanced, it's important not to look at friendships as transactional. A transactional relationship is one where people do nice things only so they can get something in return. This might look like someone spending money on their friend, expecting them to return that kindness with attention and loyalty. Approaching friendships with this mindset will eventually lead to disappointment and resentment. Instead, find and be the type of friend who naturally encourages and uplifts simply because they want to.

> **They make sure you see the good in yourself.** Good friends and family will point out your strengths and the things you are good at. Instead of hounding you about your unique abilities or being jealous of your skills, they will want you to succeed and will look to you to feel the same about them. Look for people who are kind, supportive, and encouraging.
>
> **Positive + Positive = Positive.** When positive people hang around other positive people, they all start rubbing off on one another. You want to be part of the positive atmosphere; it will draw more people to you who are also looking for a positive atmosphere.
>
> **School can be hard.** It's sometimes hard in school when it seems like the meanest people have all the friends and are the center of attention. Negative attention doesn't last, and it doesn't build long-term relationships and friendships. No one wants to continually be around people who make them feel bad, and over time, your peers will gravitate to people who make them feel good about themselves. Be that person.

Be Kind to Yourself

> **No One Is Perfect.** One of the most important parts of having confidence and knowing your self-worth is remembering that no one is perfect. It's not worth it to beat yourself up, give yourself a hard time, or dwell on when you do make a mistake.
>
> **Be Accountable.** When you make a mistake, which will happen, you must know how to take accountability. Don't try and make excuses because mistakes are how you will learn and grow. Demonstrating accountability to others, especially when your mistake hurts someone or makes another's life more difficult, will

earn you respect and trust. After all, everyone makes mistakes—what matters is how you proceed. Once you take responsibility for your mistake, it's time to move on.

Forgive yourself for your mistakes. You've taken responsibility and acknowledged your mistake. It's time to forgive yourself. If you hold onto a mistake, it can make you feel guilty and doubt yourself and often doesn't help anyone. Mistakes are meant to happen and meant to be let go. If you have people around you who won't let you move on from a mistake, then the issue is with them and their negative feelings, not with you. Try to distance yourself from these people and don't acknowledge their opinions—they are not more important than your own opinion.

OVERCOMING SELF-DOUBT

No matter how hard you work, sometimes self-doubt might creep in. When that happens, remember:

Don't compare yourself to others. One of the easiest ways to let your confidence slip is to compare yourself to others. Everyone is going to have their strengths and weaknesses. There is nothing wrong with not being the best at something—you have your talents, and you need to focus on them.

Accept your flaws. Just like we can't all be good at everything, there will be some things that we are just bad at. In fact, having flaws is part of what makes us unique. Would you enjoy hanging out with someone who was perfect at everything? Probably not. Embrace your flaws and know that they make you a better person.

Focus on your accomplishments. Instead of focusing on your weaknesses, focus on what you have accomplished. Make a list of your recent or notable accomplishments. Paying attention to what you have done right lets you move past what you haven't done perfectly.

CHAPTER THREE:
IMPORTANT LIFE SKILLS

One of the most important parts of growing up is learning to become independent, which allows you to have a more successful and fulfilling life. Here are some basic skills you should make sure to master so you won't have to rely on other people to take care of you while also being able to take care of others.

BASIC COOKING SKILLS

Knowing how to cook for yourself and others is a huge part of being an adult. No one wants to live off fast food or frozen dinners forever. It's great for a treat, but a long-term diet of those foods can lead to health problems. Knowing how to cook is a great way to impress people and show off another skill set.

Food Safety:

There are bacteria on certain foods that you won't be able to see or smell. You won't even taste the bacteria when you eat the food. The only way to keep these harmful bacteria from being in the food you eat is to follow food safety rules.

> **Clean:** Make sure you clean your food prep area and wash your hands for at least twenty seconds before touching food. While cooking, clean your cooking surfaces regularly and wash your hands every time you handle raw meat.
>
> **Separate:** Keep your raw fish, meat, and poultry separate until you are ready to cook, and keep your cooked and uncooked foods apart. Don't forget about the meat juices that can also carry bacteria. Always clean up after your raw meats. Be sure to check the best-by dates. If food is out of date, then it isn't safe and needs to be thrown away.

Cook: Meat and eggs have a temperature they must reach before they are considered safe.

- Eggs and ground meat need to be cooked to 160°F
- Chicken and other fowl need to be cooked to 165°F
- Beef needs to hit at least 115°F, but closer to 140°F for medium and 160°F for well-done
- Pork, chops, steaks, or ham needs to be cooked to at least 145°F

Cold: Keep food properly refrigerated, as leaving food at room temperature allows harmful bacteria to grow even if it is cooked. Always put food in the refrigerator within two hours of it being cooked. Don't leave it out for longer than that.

Holding a Knife Properly:

When using a kitchen knife, you should ensure the knife is sharp. Lopping off a finger is the last thing you want to do while preparing dinner. Grip the handle firmly and make sure your fingers are behind the guard between the blade and handle. With your other hand, make a claw, tucking the tips of your fingers in. This allows you to hold your food without cutting off the tips of your fingers. Use your knuckle against the knife to guide the cut of the food. Start slowly—the more comfortable you get after lots of practice, the more quickly you'll be able to go.

Different Types of Cuts:

Slice: You slice something when you cut a piece of large solid food, such as cheese or bread.

Julienne: You would cut vegetables into very thin slices. In a recipe, you might see an instruction to julienne peppers or cabbages.

Dice: Cut food into small pieces that are all perfectly square and the same size. No one gets it right away; the food is still good, even if it isn't perfect. You might dice an onion.

Mincing: Mincing is a lot like dicing, but you cut them even smaller into teeny, tiny pieces. You might mince garlic to add to a dish.

Chop: Chopping is just cutting things smaller, but they don't have to be the perfect size — just roughly chopped up. You chop up lettuce for a salad.

There are more cutting terms you might come across, but they are in much more advanced recipes and will take time to perfect. Starting with the basics will do the job.

How to Boil Water:

Boiling water is one of the most basic skills you'll use while cooking. All you must do is fill a pot half full and place it on the stove. If you overfill it, it will boil over. Turn the heat to medium-high (7-8 on a 10-point scale) and give it time to go from still to forming little bubbles (simmering) to a rolling boil. If you can boil water, you will always be able to fix food for yourself.

Pasta: After your water comes to a boil, add salt and then pasta; cook for six to eight minutes until the pasta is al dente, then drain your pasta. Al dente means that your pasta is soft and not hard but still has a little hardness in the center.

Rice: When you are cooking white rice, make sure you always rinse it first. You'll need water in a pot with a little bit of salt at a two-to-one ratio (this means two parts liquid to one part rice). For an extra flavor boost, use chicken stock, beef stock, or vegetable stock instead of water. This is what a lot of restaurants do when they make seasoned rice. Bring your liquid to a boil; once it's rolling, turn it down to low and add rice. Put a top on the pot and cook until all the water is absorbed, for about fifteen minutes. Once it's done, let the pot sit for eight to ten minutes. Then fluff the rice with a fork, and you're done!

Eggs: Boiled eggs are a great source of protein and can be used as a snack, as a topper for salad, or to make a sandwich spread. Put an inch or two of water in a pot with two eggs. Turn to high and bring to a rolling boil. Turn to the lowest setting and cover the pot. Let the eggs cook for nine minutes. Then, remove the eggs and place them into a bowl of cold water. Add or reduce time to suit what firmness you want for your eggs.

- 3 minutes for a soft, gooey yolk and barely hard white
- 4 minutes for a kind of gooey yolk and hard white
- 5 minutes for a medium-cooked, not gooey, not hard, and hard white
- 7 minutes for hard-boiled with a fluffy yolk
- 9 minutes extra hard-boiled with it hard all the way through

Other Ways to Cook:

You might see some other terms when trying to find something to cook. Here are the most common cooking methods you may come across.

Baking: When you are instructed to bake something, you'll be putting it in the oven to bake it from the top and bottom. The most common foods that you'll be baking are bread, cakes, pies, cookies, and casseroles. Baking is a great skill that can really let you be creative and try out different flavors and flavor combinations.

Broiling: This method also involves the oven, but instead of the power coming from the inside of the oven, high levels of heat will come directly from the top of the oven. Broiling can be done in the oven using the broil setting. It can be used to cook meats, fish, and some vegetables. Make sure to use a pan that can handle high heat.

Frying: To begin frying, you'll need oil such as olive oil, vegetable oil, peanut oil, avocado oil, or coconut oil. Begin by heating the oil in a frying pan on the stovetop. Once the oil is hot, place the food directly in the oil and let it cook. Some of the most common fried foods are fried chicken, fried fish, French fries, onion rings, fried green tomatoes, and fried pickles. Keep in mind that once the oil is hot, it might start "popping" or sending off tiny hot oil missiles around the stove. These will burn you! If any kind of liquid or ice hits that hot grease, there will be lots of popping.

Grilling: To grill food, you either do it outside with charcoal (or gas) or with an indoor electric countertop grill. It's a healthy way to cook meats, fish, and vegetables. If you are cooking outdoors, make sure to have a well-ventilated area and clean your grates before you grill. Make sure that whatever grill you are using gets hot enough before you start grilling. When using charcoal, the coals must burn for a little while to avoid leaving a chemical taste on your food.

Roasting: Roasting is also done in the oven and involves heating from below. Roasting works for meats and vegetables and is especially useful for cooking potatoes. For simple roasted potatoes, preheat the oven to 425°F, scrub potatoes, chop them into one-inch cubes, and grease a pan. Then, in a bowl, put potatoes, a little bit of oil, onion powder, salt, pepper, paprika, and parsley, and coat the potatoes well. Lay them in a single layer on the pan and bake for forty minutes.

Sautéing: When you are sautéing something, you are cooking it on the stove in a pan with a little bit of oil. This method is often used to cook vegetables.

Steaming: This can be done on the stove or in the microwave and is basically cooking with heated water and letting the steam do the work. Steamed vegetables are healthy and a great option. Vegetables can be bought in steamer bags from the frozen area so they can be popped into the microwave with no mess, no fuss, just a quick, easy snack.

Using a Recipe

A recipe tells you how to cook something, and it will include an ingredient list and directions. Always read through the ingredients and lay everything out that you will need, including tools and ingredients. Then, read the directions and make sure to reread them because you want to know exactly what steps are involved. Go ahead and preset your oven if you will be using it so that it will have time to heat up to temperature.

While going over your ingredient list, you will see different measurements indicated. When you are using measuring cups, over-fill them and scrape them off level to make sure you get the correct amount. You don't want to pack the ingredients but rather leave them loose.

Most likely, the only ingredient that you'll ever pack down will be brown sugar. You must pack brown sugar tightly in the measuring cup to get the correct amount.

Fluid is measured in fluid ounces and will require a liquid measuring cup. Make sure to use the correct measuring cup for both wet and dry ingredients.

MONEY MANAGEMENT AND BUDGETING

Money management is a skill that will allow you to accomplish your long-term goals in life and enjoy short-term goals with less stress. Any big purchase requires at least some cash, and the earlier you start saving, the more you'll be able to save. As you save and set more financial goals, you will begin to better understand healthy finances.

Here are some of the common budget categories:

Needs are the most important bills you will have. They are the things that you must have to live, such as shelter, food, healthcare, transportation, and electricity.

Wants are the things that you would like but don't really need, such as the newest phone model or movie tickets.

Savings are funds you set aside to use for future purchases, such as college, a car, or a first house. Savings are also necessary to create a safety net for yourself in case life throws something unexpected your way, like an injury, job loss, speeding ticket, or home repair.

Here are some different budgeting strategies:

50/30/20: This method is very simple: You will take your paycheck, allowance, or earned money and use 50% for any needs or bills, 30% for wants, and 20% for savings. This method ensures that you are not overspending in any category. This method might not be feasible when you're first starting out. For example, if you are a young person without significant familial support, it is not always guaranteed that your income will be double your housing costs at first. If this is the case, don't freak out. Instead, consider choosing one of the other budgeting systems for the time being, or think about moving to a cheaper area, getting a roommate, or living with your parents for a bit while you establish yourself.

Zero-Based Budgeting: To use this method, you would start at zero and list out all your bills. Add them up, and if they come to more than your income, you must go back and decide what's least important. Usually, items in our want categories are first to go. Imagine you are having a party with $100 to spend. You figure $50 for food, $25 for decorations, $15 for games, and $15 for balloons. You've gone over your $100, so you'll have to cut somewhere. You might decide to cut the $5 off the balloons because they are a want for the party, not a need. You can still have the party without balloons.

Envelope System: With this system, you take all your available funds and separate them into labeled envelopes. Each envelope should be labeled food, fun, savings, clothes, gas, insurance, rent, and any other category you regularly spend money on. Once the envelope is empty, you can't spend any more money on those things. If there is money left over at the end of the month, you add it to the next month.

Pay-Yourself First: The goal of this way of budgeting is to focus on your financial future. When you receive money, you put a set amount into savings first thing. To figure out how much you need as the pay-yourself-first amount, make a list of your income, a list of your fixed bills (needs), and a list of wanted expenses. Subtract your fixed bills from your income and then decide how much of that is needed for your wants and how much can go into savings.

Money management is an important life skill, and the earlier that you learn it, the better you will be able to tackle life as you get older. Start saving now.

In addition to traditional savings, if you have the flexibility, it is a great idea to consider investing at a young age. Look into putting away some money into a low-risk index fund, treasury bonds, or a Roth IRA to begin building an investment portfolio and making passive income. While not without risk, investments can be a huge part of building financial independence. Remember that the earlier you start investing, the more money you stand to make over time. Like savings, even small amounts of money invested consistently and in trustworthy sources can compound significantly over time, offering more financial freedom than a traditional savings account.

TIME MANAGEMENT AND ORGANIZATION

Another important skill you should start working on now is time management. There is only so much time in a day, and to get the most out of it, you should have it organized and planned. With a good time management system, you should get more done in less time. Below are different methods that work for some people, but don't be scared to come up with your own method or modify one of the following strategies:

> **Task Ranking:** This is a great way to handle your time when you've got an overwhelming list of things to do. Start with making a list of all the tasks you need to accomplish in a set amount of time. Prioritize them from most important to least important. Next, tackle the most important task first, working your way down to the least important. Some ways to make this technique work better for you would be to break down the tasks into shorter tasks, use a timer to see how fast you can get them

done, and have a reward planned for once you accomplish your goal. The hardest task is often what keeps us from getting our to-do list done, so getting it out of the way can move the entire process along.

Time Blocking: This method of time management involves breaking your day into different groups and assigning each block to a specific task or activity. For example, instead of working on your homework a little in the morning, a little right after school, and a little before bed, consider creating a set "block" of time during the day designated exclusively to homework. Other blocks might include chores, exercise, family time, organizing for the next day, and so on. Next, make sure you're sticking to the time limits you place for yourself on each category of activity to ensure that you're taking consistent care of all your needs equally. If you get easily distracted or get stuck on a project, this is a good method for you because it limits the amount of time you have for each task. You don't have to have an entire day to fill with blocks of time; it can just be for after school or on the weekends if that is all the time you have available. This planning strategy lets you plan your day in advance to make sure that you are using your time in the most effective way possible. However, this method does not work for everyone, and starting out, you might find that you have trouble getting the right amount of time for the right tasks. Give yourself a few weeks to see if it works, and if not, move on to another method.

Rapid Results Plan: This is the rapid planning method and is helpful for prioritizing tasks that need your immediate attention. The first step is knowing what your most important task is and what you want the results to be. Maybe it's getting some weightlifting time in for a sport or studying for your math exam. The second step means you are going to put those tasks first and then list the rest of your tasks by level of importance, deciding what the purpose of each task is and how important it is to you.

The third step is all about coming up with how you are going to accomplish your most important tasks and planning to get it all done. This method is all about achieving your most important goals first and getting them completed quickly so that you don't have to continue to worry and can move on to the rest of your day.

30-Minute Attack: This is a great way to manage your time if you do well with working hard in short bursts followed by a break. This technique focuses on using thirty minutes at a time to work hard on whatever task you need to accomplish. At the end of your thirty minutes, you take a five-minute break. This allows you a moment to reset and then start again. After four thirty-minute segments, you take a longer break, maybe ten or fifteen minutes. It's another great time management system to help keep distractions at bay and will be especially useful for studying and not getting bogged down in all the information. Just have a timer handy and get to work.

Rationing Time: Rationing time means that your task will take the amount of time you give it to complete. In other words, if you give a task a shorter time frame, you will complete it in that shorter time frame. If you give it longer, it will take longer to finish. This means if you have a project due in a week and you set your deadline to the night before, that's when you will finish your project. However, if you set the deadline three days before, that's when you'll finish your project. It works well if you break down the larger tasks into smaller tasks and focus on accomplishing those by a set deadline. Make sure your deadlines are realistic, or you'll get discouraged.

Visualizing Time: This makes it easier to visually see what needs to be done. To use this method effectively, you need to write your schedule down and sort all the tasks you want to accomplish into four categories. The four are **Urgent** (important tasks that should be focused on first), **important but not urgent** (tasks that you can complete later), **not important but urgent** (these tasks have a quickly approaching deadline but don't need your entire attention), and **not important and not urgent** (tasks you can probably remove from your list). Being able to see everything you want accomplished broken down into these categories allows you to come up with an action plan.

Try whichever time management technique you think will work for you. The most important part of any strategy is to stick with it. It's okay to be flexible, but don't let yourself off the hook if you've slacked off or fooled around instead of completing the tasks you set as important.

Time management is a skill that will make life so much easier when you are in college or working full-time.

COMMUNICATION AND SOCIAL SKILLS

Time management and money management are great skills, but sometimes, the ability to communicate with people is an even better skill to have. Practicing the following strategies will allow you to become a master at communicating with others and developing your social skills.

Active Listening: This is a big one for both your friends and the adults in your life. When someone is talking to you, make sure to actively follow along. It might mean nodding to show you are listening, asking questions, or making eye contact. These small actions let the speaker know that you care about what they are saying and that they are important to you.

Respect Opinions: Everyone has an opinion about most things. Their opinion doesn't have to agree with yours—sometimes, it's enough to acknowledge that you have different opinions and move on. No matter how wrong you think someone else's opinion is, you should never attack them or behave cruelly toward them. It is great to stand up for what you believe in, and part of being an independent, critically-minded adult is feeling comfortable challenging ideas that might be harmful, oppressive, or toxic. However, resorting to personal attacks and aggression is not productive. Think about how you would feel if someone didn't listen to your opinion or made you feel dumb about it.

Body Language: You don't have to walk around grinning all the time, but being aware of the look on your face can go a long way to making your look approachable and nice. Scowling can make people less comfortable talking to you. Try to stand up straight, not slouch, and keep a pleasant look on your face while communicating with people.

Stay Positive: No one likes a "Negative Ned". If all you have to say is negative responses, then stay quiet, or better yet, think of a positive way to respond. For instance, if your friend makes the comment, "I can't believe our football team lost the game last night," instead of responding, "I'm not surprised, they always lose, they stink," try instead, "They are working hard, I bet they'll win next week." It makes you a more cheerful person to be around and makes people feel good instead of bringing down the atmosphere.

CHAPTER FOUR:
NAVIGATING FRIENDSHIPS

It can be hard to keep friendships at this age because everyone is changing their opinions, habits, identities, likes, and interests. Making new friends and working to keep old ones can be a challenge, but here are some ways that make it easier.

MAKING NEW FRIENDS

No matter your age, making new friends can be difficult, but the most important thing you can do is be yourself. Friendships that make you feel like you must fake it are not the kind of long-term friendships you want.

Being a good listener and using some of those skills we talked about earlier is an important part of making new friends. It is okay to talk about yourself, but make sure you make time to let other people talk about themselves too. No one wants to hang out with a friend who doesn't care about what they have to say. The same goes for you. If you have a friend who won't let you talk and express yourself, it might be time to make some new friends. Friendship is about supporting one another, and listening is a very important part of that.

Don't be scared to start a conversation. If you are standing in line with someone, find something to talk to them about. If you are seated next to someone new in class, introduce yourself. If you see someone looking for a seat at lunch, invite them to sit with you. People want to make friends but are often too shy to be the ones to start conversations. If you take the initiative, this will show that you are friendly and confident.

This time of your life will open so many opportunities to try new things and new experiences. Don't be afraid, because you might meet someone who has the same passions that you do and who would make a great new friend.

No matter where you are, there are opportunities to make new friends, even when you are away at camp or on a trip. Long-distance friends are great for pen pals, social media friends, and phone call chats. You never know where you will wind up down the road, and having friends in lots of places means you might be closer to them one day during or after college.

MAINTAINING LONG-TERM FRIENDSHIPS

Once you have become friends with someone, it's easy to grow that friendship if you are in the same class or activity together. But what do you do when you don't see each other every day anymore?

One of the fastest ways to lose a friendship is to fail to keep up communications. Lack of communication will cause a friendship to fizzle out and the two of you to drift apart. Sometimes, all it takes is a quick text, phone call, or message to stay in touch. However, you should make time to do things together as well, even if it's just a few hours hanging out one Sunday once in a while or via video call. That time together is what will cement the friendship and build a lifelong connection.

You can also lose friends if you aren't supportive. If a friend is going through a hard time, that means you need to focus on them. Spend some time listening to them and understanding what they are going through. The best friends stick together through thick and thin. Just like you would want someone there for you if something upsetting is going on in your life, be there for your friends.

True friends don't lie to each other. Honesty is a valuable trait to have in a friend. Sometimes, best friends must be honest even when no one else is, and you need that person you can count on and call anytime. Don't take your friendships for granted by telling falsehoods or spreading misinformation—no friend will appreciate that. Your real friends will like you just as you are.

Having friends is like growing a tree. If you take the time to nurture and fertilize your tree, it will grow into a healthy, large tree. If you don't take care of it, it might still grow, but it'll be sickly and a less-than-great version of itself. Friendships make your life better, so invest in them.

DEALING WITH CONFLICT IN FRIENDSHIPS

No matter how great a friendship is or how close the two of you are, there will be times when conflict arises. It's natural and a part of the growing process. If you want your friendship to become a life-long friendship, then understanding how to resolve conflict is essential.

When conflict arises, it's important to remember that there are two sides to every story. Just because you feel like you are in the right doesn't mean you shouldn't listen to your friend's viewpoint as well. Communication is the key to handling conflict between friends.

If you were in the wrong, the first step to resolving conflict is to admit you made a mistake and acknowledge that you might have hurt your friend. Real friendships have forgiveness built in.

Talk It Out:

Oftentimes, the other person will think you are in the wrong, and you'll think they are in the wrong. Sitting down and explaining your perspective to one another can help both of you understand the other's point of view. No one has to be right, and no one has to be wrong. It's important to understand that sometimes the fight is just a misunderstanding, and talking will resolve it.

Set boundaries. By talking it out, you might discover there are some things your friend doesn't want to talk about or mention, and maybe this lack of boundaries leads to you unintentionally hurting your friend's feelings (or vice versa) in the first place. While talking and figuring out how the argument started, you can set boundaries with each other.

Be willing to forgive. The last step to resolving a conflict is to let go of hurt feelings and anger you might be carrying. Holding onto those feelings after talking and apologizing is just asking for resentment to fester in your friendship, which will do neither of you any good. If you want to keep your friend, you must let go of the negative feelings.

Take a break. If nothing else has worked and there are still hurt feelings and anger, it might be time to take a break. Taking a break doesn't mean you are done being friends. It just means that, for now, you need a little space. Having that space can help you decide what you want to do next and how or if you want to move forward. Cool down and make decisions with a level head.

Remember, everyone makes mistakes. You must be willing to forgive them and to let go of grudges.

UNDERSTANDING THE VALUE OF FRIENDSHIP

You can't put a price on friendship—it is one of the most valuable things in life. Having the support and understanding of friends can make all the difference in the world through both good and bad times. It's important to have people who will celebrate your successes with you and stand by you if you fail.

Studies also show that friendship can help cope with stress, increase happiness, and improve your well-being.

Not all friends will be the same. You'll have friends who are your confidants that you can talk to about anything and trust with your deepest secrets. There will be friends that you enjoy having a good time with and doing things with, and your friendship might revolve less around sharing secrets or having deep conversations. In fact, they might be more about simply enjoying each other's company.

Here are some of the many benefits of friendship:

> **Friends provide us with emotional support.** Whether you're sad, happy, or angry, they'll listen to you and be there for the important moments in life.
>
> **Friends allow us to share deep thoughts and secrets safely.** Having a good friend that you can trust means having a sounding board when you need to talk things out or solve a problem.
>
> **Friends are a source of companionship and fun times.** Some friends are best at showing you when you need to go do something fun, laugh, and maybe forget a bad day.
>
> **Friends help us deal with stress** and keep us focused on the positive things in life. Without a good support system, stress can become overwhelming.
>
> **Being part of a friend group gives you a sense of community.** It can become a second family.
>
> **Friends prevent loneliness.** You never have to feel alone if you have some friends or one really good friend to call on.
>
> **Friendships make our lives happier** and healthier.

CHAPTER FIVE: UNDERSTANDING PEER PRESSURE

Everyone feels the need to fit in and not stand out, but being part of the crowd can take away from the amazing, unique person that you are.

RECOGNIZING PEER PRESSURE

While it can be overwhelming, peer pressure is part of life. It is the influence that friends or people you are around have on the decisions you make and how you feel or behave. Sometimes it can be positive, but oftentimes, it is negative.

Knowing what peer pressure is will allow you to make better decisions instead of being guided just by what everyone else does.

The most obvious sign of peer pressure is feeling like you must do something even though you really don't want to. If you are being pushed to do something that doesn't feel right or makes you feel anxious, this is peer pressure. You don't have to give in to the urges of others. It might not be verbal peer pressure; a lot of times, peer pressure comes from silent or unspoken actions.

If you are afraid of what other people will think about you, then you are probably reacting to peer pressure. You will notice what your friends are doing and naturally want to fit in by doing the same stuff, but if you think it's wrong or it goes against your personal moral beliefs, walk away.

When your body is having reactions that make you jumpy, nervous, anxious, or uncomfortable, then it's important to listen to your gut and avoid participating in that nonsense.

If for any reason you ever feel guilty or ashamed, then it's a good idea to go talk to a trusted adult about what has happened.

While it's not always easy to stay true to yourself, don't be afraid to stand up for your needs.

STRATEGIES TO RESIST PEER PRESSURE

Setting boundaries is a great way to get ahead of peer pressure. If you let your friend know ahead of time that you aren't going to be comfortable with certain things, then they are less likely to push you on the matter.

For example, if you find out your friends are planning to skip class, let them know ahead of time that you don't want to miss any class or have make-up work. Laugh it off as something dumb they can do, but it's behavior that doesn't interest you. If they continue to give you a hard time, they probably aren't your friends. In fact, you should think about distancing yourself from those people and finding some real friends.

You don't have to hang around with people who push you to participate in things that make you uncomfortable. Join another group of people via sports, after-school clubs, a local youth group, an art club, music group, or a volunteer program. These will be people you can find new ways to connect with that don't leave you questioning your choices or your morals.

Remember, this is the time you establish what you think is right and wrong. Stick to it and refuse to let other people decide for you. You are still the same person on the inside, even though your body is changing. Don't let the changes you're going through or other people are going through make you forget who you are.

Keep in mind that everyone feels peer pressure in one form or another. If at any point it feels like more than you can handle or more stress than you know how to deal with, find your trusted adult and let them know how you are feeling. For example, if a friend is asking to cheat off you on a test and you aren't comfortable with that, then let them know. If they continue to push you, then let either tell your teacher or another adult you can trust. You don't have to get anyone in trouble; just let them know you would be more comfortable sitting elsewhere.

As you are struggling with these issues, so are your friends and classmates. If you see someone being pushed, pressured, or bullied, do not hesitate to step in and support them. It makes a world of difference when one person will stand beside you doing what you feel in your gut is right.

THE ROLE OF ASSERTIVENESS

Assertiveness means that you can be direct, clear, and confident. When you assert yourself, you can stand up for your rights and needs without being overbearing. Assertiveness is an important skill to have, especially right now, when you are trying to establish who you want to be and how you want to handle things.

There are some benefits to being assertive:

> **More people will take you seriously**, and you will be able to communicate with your parents and other adults in a respectful manner about what you need or want.
>
> **You stand a better chance of getting what you want.**
>
> **Being direct can allow you to resolve conflicts peacefully** with less emotional upset.
>
> **Your relationships with both family and friends** will become healthier.

Assertiveness sets you up to be successful in school and later in life.

That all sounds great, but how do you act assertively? Here are some tips:

Be aware of what you want or need. If you know yourself, you can stand up for yourself.

Have confidence. As we talked about earlier, confidence can make all the difference.

Be direct in your communication and be clear about where you stand.

Being assertive is not being disrespectful. While standing up for yourself, be aware of others and what their needs and wants are as well.

Don't let your assertiveness become aggressive. If you are making other people uncomfortable, then you are being aggressive, and you need to dial it back. Don't be demanding, be clear.

Be persistent when you are trying to communicate. It sometimes takes time for people to recognize what you are saying. Don't give up.

This is a skill you must work on, but it is well worth the effort in the long run.

LEARNING FROM PEER PRESSURE EXPERIENCES

Not all peer pressure is negative—sometimes, it can be a positive thing. When you surround yourself with positive, goal-oriented people, you push each other to do better and work harder. Do not focus on things that will drag you down.

Something as simple as the way we eat can be influenced by the people we hang around. For example, if all your friends eat junk food every time you hang around each other, then you are more likely to eat junk food as well. If you hang around friends who make healthier decisions for their bodies and eat better, you are more likely to, as well. These healthy decisions make you a better athlete, make focusing easier, and motivation higher. However, make sure you aren't following your friends' choices to any extremes—restricting necessary calories, over-exercising, and body-shaming are all behaviors that could have long-term consequences on your mental and physical health. Adolescent boys and girls alike can put unhealthy pressure on themselves to look, work out, and eat a certain way. It's important not to let other peoples' body image ideals pressure you into taking unhealthy steps to fit in. Focus on making the best choices for your body, recognizing that everyone has different physical health needs and limits.

Being around motivated people who have short- and long-term goals makes it easier for you to set goals and work toward them. Planning for college gets easier when your friends are doing it as well. If you don't have friends who are motivated to set goals, then you can be the positive influence that encourages and sets the example for everyone.

A place where you might see positive peer pressure is on sports teams. It only takes a few people wanting to win and working as hard as they can to encourage the rest of the team to do the same. Two people can't win a game by themselves (unless it's doubles tennis!), but two people can encourage the other ten people to win the game.

You can ace your test, but it can be much easier when a group of your friends study together because you all want to get good grades. Pushing each other to study together is another form of positive peer pressure.

Positive peer pressure doesn't only have to come from your friends, but having a good role model can also pressure you to succeed. It might be a parent, a coach, a teacher, a historical role model, or a famous person— as long as looking at them makes you want to do better and work harder.

Always be kind and respectful, but don't be scared to help push your friends and yourself into better habits, tasks, and plans.

Finally, never forget to ask for help. If you're struggling with peer pressure, reach out to your doctor, school counselor, or a trusted adult.

CHAPTER SIX: PHYSICAL HEALTH AND FITNESS

Physical health is important as you journey through all the changes puberty will bring. Let's talk about what it takes to stay physically healthy.

IMPORTANCE OF EXERCISE AND FITNESS

Exercise and fitness are going to be very important during your life, and the teen years are a good time to start having good habits that will carry you through your adult years.

Staying active can help improve your cardiovascular health, which in turn can reduce the chance of heart problems later in life, such as stroke, heart disease, heart attacks, or high blood pressure.

Being active will also help you build stronger bones and muscles, which is very important as your body goes through its rapid growth. Not only will it help build stronger bones and muscles, but it will improve your coordination and balance.

When you are active, you are less likely to develop health risks such as heart disease, high cholesterol, diabetes, cancer, joint pain, anxiety, and depression. If you are currently struggling with any of these conditions, talk to your doctor. They can help you create a game plan for a healthier lifestyle. There are also registered dietitians who can help you create a meal plan that works best for your age, body, and lifestyle.

Exercise will also help with your mental health and mood. When you are active, your body releases endorphins that will boost your mood and make you happier. Getting exercise will also help you sleep more deeply, which contributes to a better mood. As a teen, stress will be a part of growing up and can be overwhelming. Exercise is a great way to combat stress naturally because exercise causes cortisol levels to decrease. The lower cortisol levels lead to less stress and anxiety. Add some music or a podcast to your exercise routine, get outside if the weather permits, and let your energy propel you forward.

Exercise is a great way to boost your endorphins, get better sleep, help with stress or anxiety, and, as a result, improve your self-esteem and confidence. It will also increase your energy levels, which allows you to do better in school and other activities. Exercise increases blood flow, which leads to you feeling more alert and positive.

Try to spend at least thirty minutes a day exercising. Some great exercises include team sports like soccer, basketball, or baseball and individual sports like running, swimming, and biking. Other great ways to exercise include martial arts, yoga, hiking, or even camping if you are carrying your gear.

HEALTHY EATING HABITS

One of the most important parts of learning how to eat healthily is learning about food groups and how much of each you should be eating each day.

Fruit

You should be eating at least four servings of fruit a day. Make sure that the fruit you are eating doesn't have added sugar. For example, a cup of fruit cocktail has a lot of additional sugar to make it sweeter, and fruit juices can have plenty of sugar added. Sometimes, these added sugars can take your healthy snack and make it bad for you. To make sure you are getting the right amount, keep these serving sizes in mind:

Fruit Portion Sizes:

- A piece of fruit the size of your fist (apple, peach, or orange)
- Several small pieces of fruit combined to the size of a fist (grapes or plums)
- ½ cup of frozen or sugar-free canned fruit (frozen berries or bananas)
- ¼ cup of dried fruit (dried mangos or pineapple)
- ¼ cup of "no sugar added" juice (apple juice or pomegranate juice)

Blueberries are a great fruit to snack on since one cup of blueberries gives you a serving that is packed with fiber and vitamins. An apple also gives you a full serving of fiber and vitamins, whether you eat it as a full apple, apple sauce, or sugar-free juice.

Vegetables

Every day, you should try to have at least four servings of vegetables since they have so many vitamins, minerals, and fiber. Make sure to avoid vegetables that have sauces added, have been fried, or have been "candied." Here are the serving sizes to keep in mind:

Vegetable Portion Sizes:

- 1 cup of raw leafy greens (spinach, kale, and romaine)
- ½ cup of cooked vegetables (broccoli, carrots, cauliflower)
- 1 cup of no sugar added vegetable juice (tomato juice, carrot juice)
- ¼ cup of dried vegetables
- ½ cup of starchy vegetables (potatoes and corn)

Limit your starchy vegetables to one serving per day and try to focus on green vegetables. Broccoli is a great green to have on your plate because it carries such a high amount of vitamins and minerals. Kale and spinach are two other great green veggies.

Grains

Having at least three servings of healthy grains every day is ideal. Healthy grains include whole grains, such as brown rice, oats, or quinoa.

Grain Portion Sizes:

- ½ cup whole wheat pasta or rice
- 1 piece of 100% whole-wheat bread
- ½ cup of oatmeal
- 6 whole-wheat crackers
- 1 tortilla (whole wheat or corn)
- 1 cup of cereal with whole grains

Checking labels is important, as you are looking for "100% whole grain." Substituting things like whole wheat flour instead of plain white flour can make any food healthier, even foods like pancakes or muffins.

Protein

Meat, fish, and dairy are common sources of protein. Getting two servings of protein a day is enough to keep your muscles growing. The best meats to eat are lean pieces, although sources of healthy fat, like fish, should not be overlooked. Don't forget, though, that protein can come from a lot of different sources and isn't just from meat. Below is a list of protein sources with their suggested portion sizes.

Protein Portion Sizes:

- 3 oz of cooked fish or Chicken (Salmon, Tuna Steak, Chicken Breast)
- 1 Egg
- 1 cup of beans (black beans, kidney beans, soybeans)
- ½ cup of nuts (peanuts, almonds, cashews)
- 1 tablespoon of peanut butter

- ½ cup of Tofu

Protein is good for you in moderation, but not if you are eating your protein deep-fried. Anytime you can get grilled or baked protein options, that's a healthier option. Eating lean protein will also help you stay feeling fuller for a long time, so you won't be as hungry as quickly.

Dairy

Traditionally, dieticians recommend three servings of dairy a day unless you are lactose intolerant. However, modern research has found that there are many alternative sources of calcium and good fats to supplement a healthy diet in place of dairy. Getting enough calcium is important for developing strong bones. Like with all food groups, it is important to vary where you receive nutrients from, and it is more important to focus on adding in more healthy foods than it is to focus on restricting foods. Focusing on adding healthier, filling, whole foods into your diet will naturally curb your cravings for unhealthy foods while making sure you get enough nutrients to develop your body and mind.

While yogurt is a great dairy source and a quick breakfast, make sure to avoid the yogurts that are loaded with sugar. Instead, opt for Greek yogurt instead. Whole milk also contains other nutrients, including healthy fats, vitamin D, calcium, and protein. Here are some serving-size examples, but please remember to prioritize your body's natural needs over numbers.

Dairy Portion Sizes:

- 1 cup of milk (whole milk, almond milk, oat milk, or soy milk)
- 1 cup of yogurt
- 1.5 ounces of natural cheese
- ½ cup of cottage cheese
- 1 cup of ice cream

Some people have an intolerance for something called lactose, which is in most dairy products. If you find that after eating dairy, you don't feel good, talk to your doctor, and they'll be able to explain more. If you need to go lactose-free, there are plenty of options like lactose-free milk, almond milk, oat milk, soy yogurt, coconut milk yogurt, cream cheese, or even lactose-free ice cream.

Remember, not every day will be ideal, and sometimes, our hectic schedules mean that we just have to eat what we can. However, when given the choice, strive for healthy options. Your food needs will vary based on your level of physical activity, genetics, and other factors. Under-eating, especially during your most intensive growth phase, can cause long-term health complications in the same way over-eating can. Make sure you're listening to your body and striving for balance and moderation in your choices. Finally, make sure to enjoy some pizza or cake every now and again.

SLEEP AND REST: ESSENTIAL ELEMENTS OF HEALTH

Did you know the longest recorded time without sleep has been 264 hours, or about eleven days? Now, you shouldn't try to go that long without sleep. In fact, after forty-eight hours without sleep, you start having what's called sleep deprivation. Your brain will stop working well, and your body won't be able to repair itself.

Sleep is important for restoring and repairing your body.

While you are in a deep sleep, the blood flow in your body increases, which allows more oxygen to your muscles and promotes healing. Your body also releases hormones, proteins, and enzymes, which allow your body to continue to grow to its fullest potential and repair the wear and tear of the day.

Saves Memories: At night, your mind takes all the memories that you have collected during the day and transfers them into long-term memory. If you don't have enough sleep to turn those short-term memories into long-term storage, then you won't remember what you have learned during the day.

Regulating Emotions: While you are already going through so many mood changes, not having enough sleep will make mood regulation more difficult. Without enough sleep, you will get more irritable and will be more likely to struggle with anxiety or depression.

Keeps You Healthy: Sleep keeps your immune system working at its best. Without sleep, your immune system will slow down and weaken, which increases your chance of getting sick.

Makes You a Better Athlete: Without sleep, you'll become less coordinated, and your reaction time will decrease. These slow reactions mean that you aren't able to perform at peak performance.

Prevents Accidents: When you're low on sleep, you lose your decision-making skills and can experience impaired judgment. If you attempt to make decisions without sleep, then you are likely to make bad decisions.

As a teen, you need at least eight-to-ten hours of sleep a night. Without that amount of sleep, you start seeing some of the negative side effects.

Tips for getting a good night's sleep:

Start relaxing at least an hour before you want to go to sleep by turning off your electronics. Winding down before you go to sleep makes sure you have a better quality of sleep.

Avoid caffeine before bedtime because it is a stimulant that will keep you awake.

Take a hot shower and try listening to relaxing music so that you can relax your body.

Make sure that your bedroom is dark, quiet, and set at a comfortable temperature.

Once you're in bed, try taking slow, deep breaths.

Set a schedule, go to bed at the same time, and get up at the same time each day so that you will have an established sleep-wake cycle.

Try keeping relaxing smells in your room, like a candle or air freshener. Some smells that most people find relaxing are ylang-ylang, lavender, chamomile, valerian, and jasmine. Any scents that help relax you or smell good to you can help you get to sleep faster.

Valerian root serves as a natural sleep aid dating back to the time of Socrates. If you're having a particularly hard night and are looking for a natural sleep aid, try a valerian root supplement.

Peaceful noises like forest sounds, creeks, rain, birds, crickets, or the ocean through a sound machine or your phone can help create a calm space to promote sleep. Evening meditations are also a great way to practice mindfulness and ready yourself for sleep.

PREVENTING COMMON SPORTS INJURIES

Concussions

A concussion is a brain injury that occurs when there is trauma to the head. Football is the most well-known sport when it comes to concussions, but hockey and soccer can also be equally dangerous. If you have experienced head trauma, you should tell an adult and a doctor right away because it might be more severe than you realize. Some common signs of a concussion are dizziness, trouble balancing, blurry vision, and nausea. Also, be aware that memory loss, ringing ears, and feeling sluggish are also signs of a concussion. Symptoms may not show up right away, so stay aware and alert someone if you have any symptoms. It can take seven to ten days to recover from a concussion and, in some cases, a month or longer. Try to stay away from screens, bright lights, and excessive movement while recovering.

Neck Injuries

Football and ice hockey, along with rugby, wrestling, gymnastics, and basketball, can result in neck injuries. A neck injury can be something called a stinger, in which the head or neck is forced to one side. Symptoms include a pinching or burning feeling in the shoulder or in the neck. Recovery takes anywhere from a couple of hours to several weeks, depending on the severity of the injury.

A neck sprain is another common neck injury and is caused when the ligaments get stretched or torn. If the pain in your neck gets worse when you move, then you might have a sprained neck. Recovery time takes four to six weeks and needs to be looked at by a doctor. Neck injuries are serious, so if you have one, you should immediately go to a doctor or the nearest emergency room.

Whiplash is like a stinger, except it is caused by a sudden front-to-back motion that causes strain on the neck. Look for the same symptoms as the first two injuries to see if you have whiplash. Only a doctor can tell you for sure what kind of injury you are dealing with.

A neck fracture or a broken neck is a severe injury that occurs when trauma causes a fracture in the vertebrae. These injuries can occur from football, hockey, or, most commonly, diving. A broken neck can cause damage to the spinal cord, which can cause paralysis, loss of movement in limbs, or even death. Be careful anytime you are jumping into the water, and avoid going headfirst unless you are jumping off an official diving board and are properly trained in diving.

Hand Injuries

Some common hand injuries that occur in sports are sprained wrists, jammed fingers, tendinitis, or fractures. If your wrist is sore, there is a chance you have sprained it. If there is intense pain, you should check with your doctor. However, for minor pains, try resting, icing, and wrapping your wrist in a compression bandage until you can see a professional. You can find affordable wrist braces at your local drugstore.

A jammed finger often occurs in sports such as basketball when the ligaments are stretched or torn. A badly jammed finger can mean a broken finger, so getting an X-ray is the only way to know for sure what you're dealing with. If you feel pain in one of your fingers, have swelling, and have difficulty moving your finger, you have probably jammed it. For minor pain, rest the finger, ice it to help with swelling, and add compression.

Tendinitis is also a common sports injury. Tendinitis occurs when the constant use of tendons causes them to become inflamed and hurt. If you have slight swelling and soreness in your hand, take it easy and rest.

Dislocations

The most common dislocation that you might experience in sports will be a dislocated shoulder. Your shoulder can become dislocated anytime you run into something, fall, or sustain trauma to your shoulder. When the shoulder becomes dislocated, the arm bone pops out of the socket and can dislocate in any direction. If your arm is dislocated, you won't be able to move it and need to get medical attention immediately. Sometimes, the swelling from a dislocated shoulder can hide a fracture or broken bone.

Other parts of your body can become dislocated as well, like your hand, fingers, or elbows.

Sprains and Strains

These are common injuries in sports and, in most cases, are mild and will quickly clear up. Sprains are stress to the ligaments between bones, and strains are injury to the tendons that attach between muscle and bones.

When you have a sprain or a strain affecting any part of your body, the first thing to do is consult with your coach, athletic trainer, or doctor. They most likely will recommend rest, ice, compression, and elevation. Rest the area by using the hurt part of your body as little as possible. Ice it to help with inflammation or swelling, as the cold will reduce the inflammation. Compression involves wrapping the hurt area so that it has some additional support. Lastly, try to elevate the injured area at any opportunity.

While there are a lot of possible injuries associated with playing high school sports, if you follow the rules and are careful, injuries don't happen as often. Here are some ways to prevent sports injuries:

>**Always take the time to warm up** before doing anything physical. Slowly warming up your muscles and tendons allows you to avoid injury.

Stretching is one of the best things you can do when you get ready to participate in any activity. Stretch out your muscles by doing a full stretch routine that a coach or trainer can help you come up with.

If you are staying active, it's important to make sure your muscles can keep up and that your body is in prime condition. Focus on strength training and building your core.

After you are done, take time to cool down and allow your body to recover from hard physical exercise.

Getting enough sleep allows you to make good judgment calls while playing sports, which prevents you from getting hurt unnecessarily.

Drink plenty of water to keep your body in peak condition.

Make sure to follow the rules of the sports you are playing. These rules are carefully thought out, and they exist to keep you from getting hurt.

Before you start playing any sport, you should have a physical done by your doctor. This involves a quick exam that lets your doctor make sure you are fit to play and participate.

Another important part of playing sports is making sure that the gear you are wearing is fitted properly.

When playing football, helmets, shoulder pads, and mouthguards are all important parts of your uniform. If your helmet doesn't fit properly, it can move around, and instead of protecting your head, it can make injuries more significant. Make sure that your helmet doesn't move or shake around when it's on your head. The shoulder pads should cover your shoulders and fit snugly without feeling like they will fall off or obstruct your movement. A mouthguard helps make sure that you don't lose any teeth. To work properly, the mouthguard needs to fit in your mouth without restricting your breathing.

Basketball requires playing with shoes that are specifically designed to support your ankles. A turned or sprained ankle can force you out of several games. Make sure your shoes fit tightly enough so they don't shift as you run. If your shoes are so tight that it hurts while you are running, you need to go up in size. Whichever store you buy your shoes at, you should enlist a professional to fit your foot to the correct size shoe. Ankle braces might also be needed if you have had an ankle injury to prevent future sprains.

Baseball requires a batting helmet, cleats, and a protective cup. If your helmet doesn't fit correctly, it can come off and fail to provide the protection you need. Cleats are made to fit your feet tightly so that as you are running, you don't get blisters or ankle sprains. A protective cup is to protect your groin area and keep the baseball from taking you out of the game.

Soccer is another sport that has important protective gear. You wear shin guards in soccer to prevent injury from other players accidentally kicking your shin. Without properly fitted guards, you could be injured and taken out of the game. Shin guards should be loose enough not to cut off circulation but tight enough to stay in place as you are running.

All sports have equipment that you wear and use. Whether it's track, wrestling, tennis, swimming, hockey, or any other sport, make sure you are wearing equipment that fits correctly. Not only is it a safety hazard if your uniform and equipment don't fit, but it also affects how you are playing. Ill-fitting clothes or equipment can constrict your movement and make it difficult to move within your full range.

CHAPTER SEVEN: MENTAL HEALTH AWARENESS

One of the most important things you can do for yourself is learn about mental health and all the good and bad ways it can affect you. Knowing this information not only benefits you but your friends as well. Sharing healthy coping strategies and empathy with those around you can create a positive ripple effect in your immediate community.

UNDERSTANDING STRESS AND ANXIETY

During your teenage years, you will deal with new feelings. Some of the more intense ones will be stress, depression, and anxiety.

Stress is a normal feeling in reaction to challenges or demands from your everyday life. Over 60% of teens will experience stress, so you aren't alone. However, if you are stressed all the time, and you are having trouble functioning, that is not normal. You might have too much on your plate and need to look at managing what you expect yourself to handle. If you continually feel stressed, you might start to feel anxiety.

What are some symptoms of stress and anxiety? Regular headaches or stomach aches could be a sign that you are stressed. When symptoms of stress or anxiety escalate, it can also lead to difficulty concentrating, forgetfulness, irritability, and a lack of interest in your usual social activities. Talk to a trusted adult if you feel like you're dealing with any of this.

WAYS TO MANAGE STRESS

One way to manage stress is to use a journal. Journaling can help you identify the source(s) of your stress, understand your feelings about the things causing your stress, and can help you keep track of your moods and emotions.

First, decide if you are more comfortable with a digital or a physical journal. There is no wrong way to journal; the most important thing is just to set aside time each day to write down how you are feeling. If you don't know how to get started, there are guided journals available. They give you prompts to help you start writing.

Some tips for journaling:

- Write in a quiet place where you won't be bothered.
- Have a set time to write each day and spend that time writing. It might be ten or thirty minutes; just make sure to devote it to your journal.
- Your journal doesn't have to be perfect, and spelling, grammar, and punctuation do not matter.
- Be completely honest in your journal.
- Feel free to write about dreams, experiences, thoughts, memories, or even questions you wonder about.
- Journaling doesn't have to just be writing. Self-expression comes in many forms, and drawing can be one of them. Fill your journal with doodles or works of art if it expresses how you are feeling.
- If you are upset about something, try writing a letter to help you work out your feelings.

Another great technique that can help cope with anxiety is deep breathing. Take a breath in through your nose, filling your lungs completely, then slowly let the breath out. Pause for a few seconds in between each breath. This slow breathing slows your heartbeat and calms the mind. Focusing on breathing allows your mind to catch up with your day. Try practicing deep breathing for fifteen minutes each day.

If you feel like your anxiety is affecting your everyday life or reducing your quality of life, it is time to talk to your doctor. Let an adult know what is going on; they have probably dealt with stress and anxiety too.

THE IMPORTANCE OF EMOTIONAL WELL-BEING

Emotional well-being is one of the cornerstones of having a healthy and productive life. It's important to pay attention to your emotional state. One of the biggest issues that teens can face these days is depression.

There are two types of depression that teens typically run into: major depressive disorders and persistent depressive disorders. Both are serious and need treatment by a doctor. Talk therapy and other treatments can be recommended by your doctor to help you combat either one. Persistent depressive disorder often causes fewer symptoms, but they tend to last longer. Major depressive disorder causes more symptoms and can be diagnosed after just a few weeks.

Depression can be caused by prolonged stress, physical or mental abuse, trauma of any kind, fighting with family or friends, physical health issues, large changes in your life, existential and psychological stress, bullying, the death of a close family member, a relationship change, substance abuse, or just neglect from the adults in your life.

Depression can also be caused by genetics that affect the way your brain works or the influx of hormones in your body. If your depression is caused by genetics, there might not be an outside trigger. Similarly, depression, to some extent, appears to go along with certain personalities and individual constitutions. Regardless of why you are experiencing depression, know that it is nothing that should bring you shame.

Almost one in five teens can suffer from depression, whether it is a short episode or a longer condition, so don't be ashamed to communicate what is going on with you.

IDENTIFYING SIGNS OF DEPRESSION

Sadness: While it's normal to feel sad sometimes, if you notice you're sad for longer than a two-week period, then it's time to talk to someone. There is a difference between being occasionally sad because something has happened or you are having a bad day, and being so sad that you can't motivate yourself for days.

Feeling worthless: If thinking about the future makes you feel overwhelmed because it seems hopeless, or you don't think it's worth it to put effort toward your future, then something is wrong. You are a unique person with great ideas and thoughts to contribute to the world. Not caring that your grades are falling or that you've lost your place in a sport or hobby means it is time to talk to your doctor or parents.

Difficulty concentrating: Another reason you might be struggling in school while dealing with depression is not being able to concentrate. If you find your focus wandering, especially while studying or reading, then know that it is part of dealing with depression. If you suddenly find yourself struggling with concentration, along with some of these other signs, speak to your doctor.

Always feeling tired: As a teen, you need at least eight to ten hours of sleep every twenty-four hours. Due to all the rapid changes you are going through, your body needs more sleep than you did as a child. However, if even after sleeping eight to ten hours a night, you find that you are still extremely tired to the point that it's affecting your day, then stop and do a self-evaluation to try and figure out why. If there isn't a good reason, let someone know.

Being Irritable: If you find that you are irritable most of the time, then it is time to take a close look at what is causing your irritation. If you find yourself cross, outraged, or irritated without cause, then it might be a symptom of something more going on.

Lack of interest: When dealing with depression, you might find that the activities or hobbies that you enjoyed before seem like more trouble than they're worth. For example, if you have always loved fishing and suddenly it seems like a lot of trouble to get your stuff together to go try and catch fish, then you might be dealing with depression. Or if you have always been on the baseball team, but suddenly going to practice isn't worth it and just seems like too much trouble, it is probably time to communicate what you are feeling to an adult. Any adult that you trust is a good person to talk to.

Pulling away from friends and family: A sudden disinterest in being around your friends is not a good sign unless you have a reason for distancing yourself. A lack of enthusiasm when it comes to hanging out with your friends and loved ones can be a sign of depression. While it's normal to want more independence from your family as you get older and stretch your legs to find out who you are, it's not normal to suddenly have zero interest in your family. These kinds of personality changes aren't normal, regardless of how many emotional and mental changes you are going through.

Crying: Crying when you feel sad or when you've been hurt is perfectly normal. It doesn't matter if the hurt is physical or emotional; there is nothing wrong with crying to process and feel emotions. Crying is a great coping mechanism for your body when you are dealing with overwhelming emotions. When you cry, it triggers several reactions in your body, such as releasing "feel-good" or happiness chemicals like endorphins and oxytocin. These chemicals help make physical pain more manageable and alleviate emotional pain. It also starts something called the parasympathetic nervous system, which controls the body's ability to relax itself so that your body starts the relaxation process. Once you start crying, that system slows the heart rate, slows breathing, and lowers blood pressure. If you find yourself crying constantly or for no reason, though, then it's not normal, even with the changes in your hormones and body.

Changes in sleep habits: If you find yourself sleeping more than the recommended eight to ten hours, or if you find that you are suffering from insomnia, let a parent, doctor, or adult know. Getting consistent sleep is one of the most fundamental aspects of good physical and mental health.

Changes in eating: If you find that you are never hungry or have no interest in meals, then pay attention to what your body is saying. The other extreme when it comes to changes in appetite is overeating, constant eating, or cravings for certain foods. This overeating can lead to poor health and weight gain, which can make your depression even worse.

Physical Pain: You should expect some growing pains with the rapid physical changes your body is going through, but if you have chronic pain, then it might be something to talk to your doctor about. Chronic pain is pain that continues for several weeks, sometimes without relief. Pain in your joints, arms, legs, back, or stomach can all be symptoms of something more than just growth pains. Pay attention to your body and what it is trying to tell you.

WHEN AND HOW TO SEEK HELP

It can be hard to communicate to people what you are going through, and most of the symptoms that come with depression can be ignored as part of puberty. If you feel like something is wrong, be your own advocate and insist on talking to your doctor. Oftentimes, if you are suffering from several of the symptoms of depression, there might be a reason to be concerned and a way to help you feel better.

If you don't feel like your doctor is listening to you or is brushing off your concerns, talk to your parents about seeing another doctor. Find someone that you are comfortable talking to, even if they don't come to the same conclusions as you.

At the end of the day, you are responsible for your mental and physical health and need a doctor to help you stay in tip-top shape. One tool that can be beneficial for communicating with your doctor is called a mood journal. It's a journal that lets you record your mood every day, along with any symptoms you feel might be more intense than normal. This record of your feelings lets your doctor see exactly what you are dealing with, day after day, and for what periods of time.

There are several ways that your doctor might diagnose depression, including the Beck depression inventory, a health questionnaire, or the PHQ-2. All of these are ways that help your doctor determine what symptoms you might have and how extreme they are.

If you ever feel like hurting yourself, talk to someone immediately. You can't control what your brain is doing, and sometimes, you might need professional help to get back on track.

One of the best resources you can take advantage of is a mental health counselor or therapist. Relying on your friends and family for support is great, but sometimes, a trained professional is necessary. These days, therapy is available in a wide variety of ways, including virtual therapy for easy access. Similar to journaling, checking in with a therapist on a regular basis can provide an outlet for your emotions, give you strategies for managing hard times, and make you feel less alone. Ask your parents or doctor to help put you in touch with a therapist if this sounds like a resource you could benefit from.

CHAPTER EIGHT: UNDERSTANDING AND EXPRESSING EMOTIONS

When you understand your emotions, it allows you to express yourself in helpful ways that allow you to communicate with others. There are different emotions that you will experience as a teen, and you will experience them in a much more intense way.

Emotions can be wonderful things; after all, what kind of life would you have without happiness, excitement, joy, love, and amusement? But just like you must learn to deal with the positive emotions, you'll also have to learn to deal with the more challenging ones.

Even "negative" emotions like sadness, anger, fear, envy, and hurt have their place in our lives and serve their own purposes. No emotion is inherently bad. It's only our reactions to those emotions that can cause negative repercussions. No matter how intense a feeling is, it's important to learn how to process and cope with it to avoid feeling overwhelmed. One way you can do this is by remembering that your emotions do not define who you are as a person. They are completely separate from you. By acknowledging this, it makes it easier to let them pass through rather than acting on them.

RECOGNIZING DIFFERENT EMOTIONS

Sadness

Sadness can be caused by a lot of things as a teenager. Your friends might move away, you might not get on a team, your relationship might end, or you may lose someone close to you. Whatever the reason, sadness is part of life and not something you can avoid. You might find yourself crying, wanting to be alone, not interested in doing anything, or overly sensitive. Let yourself be sad, but if you feel like you can't shake it, talk to a professional.

Guilt

Feeling guilty about something is your conscious mind trying to make you second guess something you've done. It might be something like cheating on a test, lying to a friend or family member, being somewhere you know you aren't supposed to be, covering up something you've done, or saying something mean to someone. When you feel guilty, you really need to take some time to look at what is causing you to feel guilty and plan for what to do next. Guilt can be a good gauge for the choices you make. However, you may find yourself at times experiencing guilt even when you know deep down you are acting in line with your values. This can happen when you grow up listening to messages from family, religion, the media, and society in general that certain things are "wrong" or "bad." This type of guilt can be unproductive and can prevent us from feeling comfortable in our own skin. Learning to distinguish between guilt that is not your own and guilt that comes from your authentic moral center is one of the hardest parts of becoming an adult, but it is important to listen to your inner guide carefully to figure out who you are.

Worry

Worry is something that everyone feels in varying amounts. You might be worried about a test, concerned about family issues, or alarmed about upcoming tryouts. It's okay to be worried; just try not to let that worry turn into stress or anxiety. Worry normally makes itself known through feeling restless and unsettled about something that is coming up.

Resentment

Resentment can occur for many reasons and usually presents itself whenever you need to create or enforce a boundary. Sometimes, the boundaries that need to be set are with yourself and not with other people. For example, resentment can sometimes come from jealousy or feeling like you are being taken for granted. It's important to recognize when it happens and take action before it escalates and harms the relationships that are important to you.

Anger

While going through puberty, you are going to feel anger that time seems to come out of nowhere and is caused by the hormones and chemicals associated with puberty. Knowing that you are angry and need some time to calm down is important for dealing with anger. Feeling the need to shout, throw something, slam a door, or have an outburst at someone are all signs that you are feeling angry. Feeling anger is alright and a part of growing up, but you need to learn how to handle it to avoid alienating your friends and family.

Fear

You might be afraid for plenty of reasons. Fear of bugs, snakes, or public speaking are all common reasons people feel scared. There might be storms, lightning, and bad weather that can scare you. Fear is a healthy reaction that you might experience when something is potentially dangerous or alarming. However, sometimes, the things that make you scared won't hurt you, and you must work to overcome them. Other times, you should listen to your body and stay away from situations that make you fearful. If you are ever scared of a person, you should let someone know immediately, as it is not normal to fear someone.

Happiness

Happiness can come from little things, like acing a test, having ice cream, finding a shirt you like, or hanging out with a good friend. Happiness doesn't have to be something dramatic, and you should enjoy the small things as well as the big things. Some big things that might make you happy include dating someone you really like, getting a car for your birthday, welcoming a new sibling, or adopting a pet. If you find yourself smiling, then something has probably made you happy.

Contentment

Contentment comes from being happy overall and having a long-lasting feeling of joy. Contentment can come when you are getting along well with your family, have a good relationship with your friends, are expressing yourself authentically, and are doing activities that make you happy. Finding ways to embrace contentment makes your overall life happier.

Amusement

Amusement comes from a rush of adrenaline caused by good feelings. Amusement can come from hanging out with people you like, riding a roller coaster, watching a funny movie, or anything else that entertains you. Amusement can be a fleeting feeling that doesn't last long, but it's important because it gives us something to look forward to. On top of that, experiencing amusing situations makes great memories.

Motivation

Motivation drives you to accomplish your goals and to do so with a determined mind. The best kind of motivation comes from yourself and lets you accomplish all the things you want. However, motivation is something that you can create as well.

Excitement

This is the feeling we have about something we look forward to. You might get excited about the weekend or even the end of school. Excitement comes from any activity that makes you happy, you are enthusiastic about, or are anticipating. It's another positive emotion that you can look forward to, and scheduling things that you know excite you is a great way to bring this positive emotion into your day.

HEALTHY WAYS TO EXPRESS FEELINGS

There are plenty of ways that you can productively express your emotions, even your less positive ones. Talking about your feelings is one of the best ways of processing your emotions. When you express yourself, it can help you understand yourself better, get perspective, and come up with solutions. Talking about your emotions and feelings also helps you build a good support system and strong relationships with the people that are important to you.

There are plenty of different ways to express your feelings. You can talk to someone you trust, such as a friend, family member, professional, coach, or even your doctor. You can also write about your feelings in a journal. Writing down how you are feeling can help you resolve them. Expressing yourself through art, such as drawing or painting, is another way to cope with your feelings. Music is a great outlet for processing overwhelming emotions and changing your mood. Physical exercise can also help take your mind off the emotions you are dealing with.

When you are talking about your emotions, it is important to be honest and open about how you are feeling. While you are being open and honest, keep other people's feelings in mind because you want to always be respectful of others. Try to avoid blaming other people for how you feel, make sure not to use harmful language, and avoid making hurtful accusations.

Another important thing to remember when dealing with your feelings and emotions is that just because you feel something, that doesn't make it a fact. For example, you might not feel good about something or be worried about an upcoming event, but there is no need to feel overwhelmed or worried.

While trying to express yourself, it's helpful to focus on what you are feeling rather than on what you are thinking. While expressing yourself, try to avoid saying things like "I am angry" and focus on saying things like "I feel angry because I feel like you were disrespectful to me." This way of communicating helps you get your feelings across more effectively and keeps the lines of communication open.

When you are struggling to express yourself or your emotions, there are some things that might help. Try to identify what you are feeling. This is often more difficult than it seems. Oftentimes, people will say they are sad when, really, they are disappointed. Feelings of anger might be confused with humiliation or envy. Finding the right terms to express what is truly going on inside can really help with emotional processing.

Once you have identified your feelings, you can start thinking about where they come from and how you want to handle them. Make sure that if you are expressing yourself to someone, you do it in a safe and supportive environment with people who will bolster you and not tear you down.

Sometimes, our emotions stem from an issue with another person. Not everyone is comfortable with confrontation, and sometimes, it is better to let things go rather than approach them face-to-face. Even in these circumstances, you can process your emotions by journaling about them or writing a letter to the person. You don't have to give them the letter, but it helps to get it out. If you decide to give them the letter, it is recommended to wait until you've processed your emotions before taking action to avoid hasty or unnecessary conflict.

Make sure you are patient with yourself. Adults have a hard time dealing with their emotions, and they have had many more years to learn to deal with them. It takes time and effort to learn how to deal with your emotions and express your feelings effectively.

COPING WITH UNCOMFORTABLE EMOTIONS

There are different ways to cope with uncomfortable emotions to keep them from becoming overwhelming.

Sadness:

- Find a trusted person to talk to about what's making you sad.
- Use a journal to express what is causing your sadness.
- Find music that resonates with you and listen to it when you are sad.
- Do something that makes you happy, whether it's being outside or spending time with people.

Guilt

- Write a letter to yourself about what happened and why you feel guilty.
- If possible, make amends for whatever it is you feel guilty about.
- When productive, apologize so that you can let it go.
- Talk to a trusted adult about what is causing you guilt.
- Forgive yourself.

Worry

- Identify the things that are making you worry.
- Plan to deal with those things so that you don't have to keep worrying.
- Use relaxation techniques like deep breathing or meditation to help alleviate some worry.
- Talk to someone about why you are so worried and let them help you.

Resentment

- Talk to the person you've been feeling resentful about to try and understand their point of view.
- Set boundaries with the person you feel resentment towards so that you don't put yourself in a bad situation.
- Forgive the person that you are resenting—most of the time, they haven't done anything intentionally to you.
- You must be able to let go of the resentment and learn to love yourself and appreciate what you have.

Anger

- Try to exercise because physical activity can help manage anger when you feel it.
- Write about your anger or draw how it makes you feel. Getting it out helps.
- Use healthy ways to express your anger, like a sport, being creative, or joining an activity.

Fear

- Talk to someone you trust as soon as you realize you are fearful.
- If you have a phobia (a fear of something that probably won't hurt you), try writing it out in your journal.
- Face what makes you scared. For example, if you are afraid of public speaking, get involved in theater so you can work on it.
- Use deep breathing and meditation techniques to help you overcome your fear.

There are a lot of positive ways to express your feelings and deal with your emotions.

1. Be honest about your feelings
2. Focus on what you are feeling
3. Don't be negative or hurtful to other people

EMOTIONAL REGULATION SKILLS

Emotions are important, even the uncomfortable ones, because they are what makes us human. They allow us to connect with other people, learn more about ourselves, and make sound decisions. If you are struggling to express your feelings, there are plenty of things you can do to make it easier.

Here are some skills you can work on developing.

Mindfulness: This is a skill that lets you stay aware of what you're doing and thinking. Being present and meaningful in all you do and say can help you keep some control over your emotions and not overreact to situations.

Self-awareness: Staying aware of your emotions, asking yourself how you are doing, and being able to label what you are feeling makes it easier to regulate those feelings as they arise.

Cognitive reappraisal: Trying to avoid negative emotions doesn't make them go away. Look at your emotions closely, find a good way to deal with them, and consider shifting your perspective.

Stress management: Making sure you have ways to handle stress is a good step in managing your emotions. Most of the time, when you are under stress, it can intensify your emotions.

Empathy: With empathy, you can have patience and an understanding of what you and other people are going through.

Adaptability: Being able to adapt keeps sudden situational changes from causing you more stress and making your emotions spiral out of control.

Some of the most important skills you can develop are how to be honest with yourself, learning how to express your feelings, and communicating your feelings in a healthy way.

CHAPTER NINE: BALANCING SCHOOL AND EXTRACURRICULAR ACTIVITIES

This is a time in your life when you will start having many more opportunities and responsibilities. You'll add sports, hobbies, harder classes, and more social life to your schedule. It's important to dedicate your time to the right activities.

TIME MANAGEMENT STRATEGIES

Most of the same strategies and techniques you read about earlier for managing your time can also be applied to managing your time between school and extracurriculars.

Task Ranking Strategy: Prioritize and tackle the most important tasks first.

Time Blocking: Break your day into time blocks and assign each block to a task so that it's saved.

Rapid Results Plan: Prioritize tasks, list them by importance, and plan to accomplish them.

30-Minute Attack: Work hard and attack your tasks for thirty minutes, then take a short five-minute break. Get four attacks done, and then take a longer fifteen-minute break.

Rationing Time: Set deadlines for your important tasks and complete them by the deadline. Keep your deadline well ahead of an actual due date so that you are done early.

Visualizing Time: Break down tasks into four categories (urgent, important but not urgent, not important but urgent, and neither) so that you can develop a plan.

Find a method that works well for you, then stick to it and be flexible with yourself as needed.

FINDING THE RIGHT EXTRACURRICULAR ACTIVITIES

There are plenty of activities out there, and finding the right ones can be important. Being involved in extracurriculars makes your life fuller, allows you to meet more friends, and is great for college applications.

Being involved in activities also teaches you responsibility, communication skills, and leadership skills. It also gives you a community and lets you work on your teamwork skills.

So, what activities might be worth considering?

Sports:

Football: A team sport that benefits include developing strength, speed, agility, and learning teamwork. Try out for your school's team or join a local team. There are rec departments, YMCAs, and local town teams; any of these are a great place to start. However, keep in mind that tackle football may not be the safest option for a young man whose brain is still developing. Many former players, parents, and scientists have expressed concerns about the potential long-term damage that football can cause, particularly at young ages. Consider opting for flag football instead, or at the very least, ensure you are wearing the correct padding and following safety measures while you enjoy the game. If you don't want to play the sport, it's still a lot of fun to learn about the game so you can enjoy watching it.

Baseball: This is another good team sport that involves two teams competing with one another. You can develop hand-eye coordination, hitting skills, and throwing accuracy while getting exercise, working on your social skills, and making long-term friendships. Baseball is something that most schools offer, and some cities even have local teams.

Soccer: With soccer, you can learn how to communicate well with teammates and be a part of one of the most popular sports in the world. With more long-distance running, you develop endurance, agility, foot skills, and get to play a great sport. There are normally plenty of options for finding a soccer team that you want to play with. Start with your school team and then look at local teams. There are also plenty of traveling teams once you build up your skills.

Track: Track has plenty of opportunities for running both short distances and longer distances, depending on your preference. But track isn't just running—also it also involves the high jump, long jump, triple jump, and hurdles, all of which test your different skills. If you don't enjoy running, there's always shot put and discus. Both require strength to throw and the farther you can throw it, the better you are. While track doesn't require as much teamwork, you still work together to win the meet. Try out for your school track team and see if you can find something you enjoy.

Tennis: Tennis can be played as a single or as a double, depending on your preference. Tennis is great for hand-eye coordination, teaches dedication, and instills you with a strong work ethic. To get involved in tennis, lessons are a great way to start. You will need to develop the basic skills before you try to play competitively, but then you can join your school team or play at the local club.

Swimming: Swimming is a mostly solo sport that requires great dedication and motivation. It is a good sport for cardiovascular health, gives you a whole-body workout, and can also be relaxing. There are options for swim teams to join, like a club or the school team. It's also a great sport just to practice at a public pool.

There are also sports like golf, disc golf, skiing, cross country, polo, rugby, and local teams that you might want to join.

Clubs and Hobbies:

Woodworking: Woodworking involves using wood to create pieces such as furniture, cabinetry, carvings, and other objects. It's a great way to express creativity, learn problem-solving, and build something to be proud of. There are classes at schools and local clubs to get involved with. If there isn't a group to get involved with, learn from books or online and enjoy the relaxing benefits.

Computer programming: Another way to learn a valuable skill that is fun and productive is trying out computer programming. Computer programming is the process of writing code, which then tells the computer what to do. Programming is a critical thinking skill that can benefit you your entire life and can be used to create software, run video games, or complete advanced calculations. There might be classes at your school you can take or online tutorials to learn from.

Writing: Putting words on paper to express yourself, whether it's just for you or to share with others, is a relaxing and productive hobby. Sometimes, you can write stories and poems or even use writing to collect information in a way that teaches people. It improves your communication skills, lets you explore your creativity, and gets your thoughts out into the world. It's a great extracurricular activity because it's a skill you can list on your college applications and turn into a career.

Gaming: Playing video or computer games is a good pastime to have if you enjoy it. Playing games allows you to chill out, have fun, and connect with other people who have the same passion. Get a console of your choice and start trying out games to see if there is one that you love. If you get good at certain games, there are local and national competitions that you can compete in. Getting involved with gaming also helps with problem-solving skills, hand-eye coordination, and reaction time.

Cooking: There aren't many things more satisfying than cooking a good meal and being able to enjoy it or share it with others. It's a great way to learn practical skills, be creative, and bring people together. To learn cooking, you can take classes, study recipe books, watch cooking shows, or learn from experience. If you really enjoy cooking, becoming a professional chef and attending a culinary school is a great career choice.

Collecting: If you decide that you want to be a collector, there are endless things that you can collect and communities that you can get involved in. There are stamps, books, dolls, coins, jewelry, records, toys, snow globes, action figures, comic books, baseball cards, rocks, or anything else that interests you. The only thing to keep in mind is to make sure that you like what you are collecting. There may be other people who collect similar items, with whom you can create a wonderful community of people.

Photography: Taking pictures of people, things, or places lets you share your view of the world with others. Photography captures memories and shows your creativity, and all you need is a camera. You can start with your camera phone and, from there, upgrade to nicer cameras. Once you start getting really practiced, you can submit your photography for contests. To learn how to take good photos, either learn through experience or talk to an experienced photographer.

Fishing: Fishing gives you plenty of quiet time to work through your thoughts and deal with your emotions. Decide what kind of fishing you like, whether it be saltwater or freshwater fishing. There are plenty of fine points to learn about fishing, like which lures, lines, and poles to use. If you love fishing, there are careers available for the best fishers out there, but most people compete in local or state fishing tournaments. Make sure you don't fish anywhere without permission from the landowner. Going out to fish relaxes you, lets you enjoy the outdoors, and allows you to catch some dinner.

There are so many more out there, and no matter what sports, hobbies, or interests you decide are for you, make sure that you don't let your interests take over your life: everything in moderation and at the right time. Learn how to balance all the aspects of your life, and you will develop good habits that will follow you into adulthood.

SETTING BOUNDARIES AND PRIORITIES

Being a teen brings new challenges related to juggling all the new demands on your time. Between school, extracurriculars, social activities, and family time, it can be extremely difficult to find balance. It's time to set boundaries and priorities so that you don't get overwhelmed or lose connection with what's important.

Here are some tips for setting your boundaries and priorities:

> **Decide what is most important to you.** What are the most important things to you? Once you have decided what's important to you, it lets you decide how to spend your time. This might mean prioritizing your family, your spiritual or religious community, a skill, your grades, or your work. Talk to your parents, teachers, coaches, or any other adult you trust to help

formulate these goals because having someone to bounce ideas off is important.

Set realistic expectations for your schedule. Don't try to prioritize so many things that they won't realistically fit into your schedule. If you try to do everything, you won't be great at anything. Focus on what you want to succeed in.

Communicate your boundaries to the people around you. If you decide that a sport or your grades are the most important things to focus on, let the people in your life know. They should understand that the time you set aside for these activities is something that you do not take lightly, and you won't be blowing them off for anything else.

Be flexible, and don't let changes upset you. The best-made plans don't always go according to schedule. In fact, you might have to adjust your priorities as needed.

Take care of yourself and give yourself time. Do not fill your schedule so that you don't get enough sleep. Make sure to eat healthy foods and exercise regularly. Being in tip-top physical and mental health will allow you to accomplish your goals.

Some other tactics that will help with setting boundaries and prioritizing your life are creating a schedule, learning to say no, building breaks into your schedule, and asking for help if you need it.

School and grades are important, and make sure to devote the time to get the grades you need and complete any assignments. Without good grades, most other activities aren't possible.

While it's wonderful to have an active social life and spend time with friends, keep in mind that building long-term goals sometimes means missing out on social events. You must decide what you want long-term and focus on it. Limit the time you spend on social media and use your time to focus on face-to-face interactions with positive people.

Family are the people that will be part of your life forever. Don't neglect those relationships and the time you might spend with them. Put time into learning to communicate with your parents, siblings, and any extended family that you'd like to be close to.

Extracurricular activities are a great way to build skills for the future and can offer future opportunities, but don't let them overwhelm you or take over the other important aspects of your life. It's not worth stressing yourself out or losing out on time spent with family and friends. Without good grades, most extracurriculars aren't possible, and your parents, coaches, teachers, or other leaders will step in to remind you of that. Be responsible enough to prioritize the pastimes that are most important to you.

AVOIDING BURNOUT

What is burnout? Burnout is what happens when you push yourself too hard, and your body gives out. This can be mental, physical, or emotional. Burnout can happen no matter your age but can be more common in teens, mainly due to the high levels of stress and expectations placed on you.

What are some symptoms of burnout? You'll feel exhausted, distracted, irritable, tired, and have physical symptoms such as headaches.

Keep expectations for yourself realistic, and don't keep cramming more on your plate. It's okay to say no when you have enough going on. Take breaks and take care of yourself when you need to.

CHAPTER TEN: ACADEMIC SUCCESS AND PREPARING FOR THE FUTURE

The tone you set now will determine the kind of future you have. While it's not everything, academic success is very important so that you can have all the options and choices you deserve.

SETTING PERSONAL AND ACADEMIC GOALS

One of the most beneficial habits you can develop is goal setting. When you take the time to sit down and write what you want to accomplish, it makes it more likely you will succeed. Try deciding what you would like to accomplish that day, that month, or even that year.

Some personal goals you might set could be:

- Improving your physical health
- Learning a new talent or skill
- Spending more time with friends or family
- Reading a book
- Learning how to cook a new recipe

Some academic goals you might set can include:

- Improving a grade in a particular class
- Getting a good grade on an upcoming assignment
- Spending extra time studying a particular subject
- Learning something new
- Raising your overall GPA
- Making honor roll
- Getting an article published in your school or local paper

STUDY SKILLS AND LEARNING STRATEGIES

There are some great study skills that you can take advantage of to help you achieve your academic goals. Learning which ones are best for you is a great first goal.

Flashcards: Using flashcards with questions on one side and the answer on the other lets you quiz yourself.

Note-taking: When you write down information, it helps you remember it much better than just hearing it.

Active reading: Reading and highlighting important parts of your lessons can help you retain information.

Group studying: Working with your peers allows you to bounce what you are learning back and forth between the members of the group.

Charts: Using different types of charts can help you sort information and make it visual.

Everyone has different learning styles and ways they absorb information. The most common types of learning styles are visual, auditory, reading, and kinesthetic. Find which study styles help you learn the best and focus on using those techniques.

PREPARING FOR COLLEGE AND CAREER PATHS

When you are prepping for college, it's important to remember that your grades, the classes you take, and the extracurriculars you are involved in affect the college options you'll have. Start planning for college early if you know it's a path that's right for you. If you wait until the last semester of your senior year, it might be too late. The sooner you are aiming for higher grades and GPA, the easier it becomes. Getting higher grades will increase the college's interest in you, the likelihood of getting accepted into more prestigious colleges, and the chances of getting more financial help.

If you are academically confident and excited about learning, take the hardest classes you are eligible for. If you can take college-level or advanced classes and know you will be able to keep up with the workload, you should take them. Colleges like to see students who have pushed themself. That said, it's always important to know your limits and avoid taking a class you know will be too academically rigorous for you to succeed in. You should strive for a balance between pushing yourself with challenging classes (ideally in your strongest subjects) and ensuring you can earn a respectable grade in whichever class you choose.

Another great way to demonstrate college readiness is by building up your college resume with extracurriculars. College admissions know that those activities develop leadership skills, let you learn teamwork, and improve communication skills.

Try volunteering in your community at places like the animal shelter, local church, or youth sports. Not only do these activities let you experience different environments, which might help you decide what you want to do with your life, but colleges want students who are going to be positive influences on their campuses. If you don't want to volunteer, try getting a part-time job. It's just another way to show colleges that you are experienced, especially if you can find an internship in the field you want to pursue.

Research colleges so that you know what your goals are and where your ideal academic future lies. The career you want to pursue is a huge factor in what college you want to attend. Also, be sure to research scholarships ahead of time, as there are so many available, and knowing what they are is vital. Scholarship opportunities include writing contests, competitions, diversity statements, and more.

Knowing what field you want to go into after college helps you decide what certification or degree you should earn. Having a long-term plan gets you to the finish line more quickly and avoids wasting your time and money.

Remember, getting into the college of your choice can be the first step in planning your career, so make sure to follow these steps:

- Start early
- Get good grades
- Take advanced courses
- Be involved in extracurriculars
- Volunteer
- Get a job (even part-time)
- Research your colleges and careers
- Apply for scholarships
- Make a plan!

EXPLORING INTERESTS AND PASSIONS

Volunteering, working part-time, and taking advanced classes can point you to a career you will love. When you are exploring your interests and find what you enjoy and are good at, you'll find what you can be passionate about. Spending high school getting experience or being involved in your future field can help you make sure that you are going in the right direction. Reach out to professionals in the field that interests you; chances are, they'd love a chance to talk to you about it.

Here are some fields and jobs you might consider:

Healthcare:

A job in healthcare has a lot of benefits. There is always demand for qualified healthcare practitioners, and the pay can be quite good. There are a lot of different routes you can take in the medical field as well, from administrator to surgeon to pharmaceutical representative. Being in the medical field gives you the chance to make a difference in people's lives, but the hours can be long and emotionally demanding. Not to mention, the time you spend getting your degrees can be longer than most. Some positions in the healthcare field are:

> **Doctor**: Treats patients and diagnosing medical problems.
>
> **Nurse:** Provides patient care and support.
>
> **Pharmacist**: Handles medication for patients and provides counseling.
>
> **Physical Therapist**: Works with patients after injury or illness to recover movement and full function.
>
> **Occupational Therapist**: Focuses on regaining skills after an injury or illness.

Business:

Business is a broad field with plenty of careers to choose from, and companies are always looking for talented employees. While you can make a good living in a business career, there are long hours, travel, and competition for positions to consider. Some positions in the business field are:

> **Financial Analyst**: Uses financial data to help make investment decisions.
>
> **Accountant:** Handles finances for individuals or companies.
>
> **Marketing Manager**: In charge of marketing and marketing plans.

Human Resources Manager: Handles the hiring, firing, and monitoring of employees.

Operations Manager: Handles the day-to-day business of a company.

Education:

Teaching gives you the opportunity to shape minds and have a positive impact on students. You traditionally get the summers off, and the hours are consistent. Teaching is a great opportunity for creativity, but it's typically not the highest-paying career field. Some positions in the education field are:

Teacher: Works helping students, grades K-12, learn different subjects.

Professor: Traditionally teaches at a college or university.

Librarian: Handles the library or collection for an institution.

Counselor: Is available to provide support and guidance to students.

Administrator: Manages a school or a school district.

Engineering:

Engineers are always in high demand, with plenty of different careers to choose from, high pay, and excellent benefits. This career allows you to make a real impact, but it's another high-stress job with long hours. There is also high competition for positions. Some positions in the engineering field are:

Mechanical Engineer: Works with mechanical devices, building, and designing.

Civil Engineer: Gets to design and build infrastructure objects.

Electrical Engineer: Handles the design of electrical systems and gets to build them.

Chemical Engineer: Focuses on designs that involve chemical processes.

Industrial Engineer: Works with companies to improve the manufacturing process.

Computer science:

Computer science or information technology is a rapidly growing field that shows no signs of slowing down. You can make a good living while putting your computer skills to work. It might be a stressful job with long hours, but there are plenty of different options. Some positions in the computer science field are:

Software Engineer: Develops software applications and maintains them on a continuous basis.

Data Scientist: Collects and analyzes data and information to use for businesses to track business.

Information Security Analyst: Works to protect computers, systems, and networks from security threats like cyber terrorism.

Network Engineer: Designs, maintains, and implements computer networks.

System Analyst: Solves business problems using analysis and information technology.

Deciding your career path should depend on your interests, skills, and personality. Take the time to do research on different fields and try to talk to people who are knowledgeable. Make an informed decision.

CHAPTER ELEVEN: SOCIAL MEDIA AND ONLINE SAFETY

With more and more social sites becoming popular, it is important to understand not only how to stay safe but how to be courteous to others.

UNDERSTANDING DIGITAL CITIZENSHIP

Being a responsible and respectful citizen in the digital world has become just as important as being a responsible and respectful citizen in the real world. Using digital devices and online tools is an important part of being online. Here are a few things to keep in mind:

- Think before you post or click.
- Don't share personal information online.
- Make sure that you are kind and respectful to other people who are online.
- Passwords are a secret that shouldn't be shared, not even with your friends.
- Do not ever share your location.

Think before you post or click. When you are online, take a minute to think before you post, comment, or share anything. Is it really something that you would want your parents, teachers, or peers to see? If not, then you need to think carefully because it can be difficult to remove negative content and impossible once someone else screenshots it.

Don't share personal information online. Personal information that should rarely be put online includes your address, full name, phone number, school name, or social security number. This information can be used by online predators or thieves to track you down or steal your identity.

Make sure that you are kind and respectful to other people who are online. Make sure that you are not flaming, trolling, or cyberbullying. Flaming is when someone uses insulting or vulgar words to attack someone. Trolling means using cruel or mean remarks to intentionally try and provoke someone. Cyberbullying is the harassment of someone online. Similar to how physical bullying is not tolerated in the real world, cyberbullying should not be tolerated in the online one. Also, there are now several states with anti-cyberbullying laws to prevent people from harassment online. When you take to the internet, be kind to other users.

Passwords are a secret that shouldn't be shared, not even with your friends. The only person who should have access to your passwords is you or, in some situations, your parents.

Do not ever share your location. Predators, criminals, and unsavory people can use your location if it is shared online to find you. If a social media site or an app asks for your location, always refuse it unless you know what it is for. GPS needs your location, but social media sites do not. Check your social media settings so that you are aware of what information you are sharing.

PRIVACY AND SECURITY ONLINE

Due to the world we live in today, it's more important than ever to protect yourself and your loved ones from crimes like identity theft, fraud, and online threats.

Privacy means keeping your personal information private, and it's not always easy. It is a right that means you should be able to control who has access to your personal information and control how it is used.

Some ways to control privacy online include:

Passwords:

Use strong passwords, don't use the same password for every account, and make sure to make it something that isn't easy to guess. If you use personal information like your birthday, name, pet's name, or favorite colors, it makes it easier for people to figure it out. Don't include anything that someone might know about you. Also, try to include an uppercase letter, symbol, and number.

Don't share the information even if you share it with your best friend because they might accidentally share it with someone you wouldn't have.

Use a password manager to your advantage and to create passwords. This is a tool that lets you randomly generate passwords that make it extremely difficult for anyone to figure out. Many password generators will save your passwords and make it easy to keep up with them.

Social Media:

Be careful about who you have as friends on social media. If you are friends with people you don't know, keep in mind that every time you post, they have an opportunity to learn more about you. If you don't know and trust them, they don't have a place on your list of friends or followers. Also, be wary of celebrities, as there are a lot of fake accounts out there.

Be mindful of what you post. Only post content that you are comfortable letting the world see. You can't take back what you expose to the world, as it will be out there years down the road. When colleges start deciding if they want you at their school and when businesses start deciding if you are a good fit for their company, they will research your social media accounts.

Avoid unknown links and attachments. If it's on social media or showing up in your email, don't click on links you are unfamiliar with because they can often lead to malicious websites. These websites are designed to infect your computer with viruses and spyware, which can lead to your computer being disabled or your personal information getting leaked.

Online Shopping:

Just because it's convenient doesn't mean it's safe. Be cautious and know who you are buying from.

Only shop websites that you know and that have the padlock icon in front of the web address, showing the site is secure.

Use a protected credit card or PayPal when shopping online. Both methods offer protection against fraud.

Never give out your credit card or PayPal information to anyone. You have no control over how often or when they might use that information.

Identity Theft:

Identity theft is a crime that can happen to anyone and has devastating consequences. When someone steals your personal information to open accounts, get credit cards, make purchases, or even get loans in your name, this is what's known as identity theft.

Protect your social security number, and never carry your card around with you. There are very few situations in which you should ever share your number online and never to an unsecured site or unknown person.

Any paperwork that has your personal information on it needs to be shredded. Don't leave it lying around in a vehicle.

Once a year after you turn eighteen, check your credit reports. You get a free report from all the major credit bureaus once a year.

The moment you see something you don't recognize on your cards, report it to your bank.

Make sure you protect your identity and your parents if you are using their information online to make purchases.

When you are trying to stay safe online, make sure to be aware of the latest online threats and stay informed. Marinating a strong firewall and purchasing antivirus software can offer you protection against accidental exposure to viruses and spyware.

THE IMPACT OF SOCIAL MEDIA ON MENTAL HEALTH

Social media has become so important in day-to-day life, and it has a huge effect on how you think, whether you realize it or not. It's important to be aware of the negative side effects of interacting with social media.

Depression: Studies have shown that higher social media usage can lead to feelings of inadequacy and depression, mainly because you start comparing yourself to the snippet of other people's lives you see online. You do not have a realistic grasp of what other people's lives are like, and seeing someone who looks like they have their life together might make you feel like you aren't good enough.

When you put yourself on social media, the negative comments can come quickly and can cause you to think negative things about yourself.

It's important to remember that online is not real life. No one posts everything that happens in their life or the mistakes that they make, even if it seems like they do.

> **Anxiety**: Another feeling that can come from overexposure to social media is anxiety because you feel that you need to constantly check for notifications.

Keep the perspective that online is not real life. Disconnect and go spend time doing something in the real world without worrying about what's going on in the online world.

Sleep Problems:

Using your phone at night can disrupt your sleep cycle and prevent you from entering a deep REM sleep, which allows your body to heal and grow. The blue light from your phone can interrupt your body's production of melatonin, which is a hormone that lets you sleep. It can also cause headaches, strain your eyes, and keep your mind from relaxing.

Attention Problems:

Using your phone constantly and multitasking between all the apps and pages can cause you to have attention problems and make it hard to focus for longer periods of time.

While social media can be a great way to connect with friends, be aware of the dangers.

Some ways to avoid the pitfalls of social media include:

> **Setting limits** and making sure that you follow them each day.

Taking breaks throughout the day and doing something else. Also, you should shut down social media (and all tech) at least an hour before going to bed.

Keep aware and take stock of how you are feeling when interacting on social media. If your self-esteem is affected or you are experiencing anything negative, talk to someone.

Stay positive and try to avoid negative people.

Never compare yourself to others. No one is perfect, no matter how much they appear online.

Always talk to someone if you need it.

DEALING WITH CYBERBULLYING

When faced with cyberbullying, it can be hard to know what to do, but here are some basic steps for handling a bully online.

Do not respond: When someone is being cruel and bullying you online, it's best if you don't engage in the behavior with them. Responding will only encourage them to continue, and reacting gives them the attention they crave.

Block any bullies: If someone has started harassing you on social media, the best thing to do is block their access to your accounts. If they don't have a way to contact you, then they can't respond to posts or send you messages.

Report, report, report: If someone is bullying you, it's time to report the bully to the site's admin. Cyberbullying is not allowed on most sites, so this could get them kicked off. Once someone is reported, and especially if they are reported multiple times, it forces the admin to remove or reprimand them.

Keep evidence: Before you delete any comments or messages you have received, save them so that you have proof if you need it later. Keep screenshots of any messages, posts, or emails. If the problem keeps going, this will protect you and make sure that the bully can't delete and deny what happened.

Talk to someone: There is no need to suffer in silence — go talk to a trusted adult about what is happening to you. Adults can offer support and might have an idea of what else will help the situation and what next steps need to be taken.

Don't neglect yourself: Make sure to take care of yourself. Simply because someone else has a negative opinion doesn't mean it's true. Get enough sleep, eat well, and exercise so that, mentally, the bullying isn't taking over.

Know you aren't alone: There are so many people who have been the victim of cyberbullying, but some resources and groups can help you with it. These groups are often present on social media and can connect you with people who understand.

Almost one half of teenagers will experience cyberbullying, and while most of those situations are harmless and can be ignored, cyberbullying can escalate quickly. Stay ahead of potential problems and stay open with your parents or another trusted adult.

Keep in mind that just because you aren't face-to-face with someone, that doesn't make your words any less hurtful. Be mindful of everything you do online so that you don't become the cyberbully.

CHAPTER TWELVE: LEARNING RESPONSIBILITY AND INDEPENDENCE

As you become older, you will notice that people will give you more responsibility and independence. It's important not to squander the chances you are given to show that you are well on your way to becoming an adult.

BECOMING SELF-RELIANT

There are some things that you can start doing now to make yourself more self-reliant:

Learning to cook. This is a life skill that shows you are ready to start taking care of yourself.

Doing your laundry. Taking care of the basics, like laundry, shows that you are maturing.

Managing your money. Creating a budget and spending limits while saving your money is another way to show you are getting ready to handle more of your life yourself.

Getting a job. Once you are old enough, get a job to make your own money, learn responsibility, and start saving for the future that you want.

Learning to drive. Knowing how to drive when you are old enough will give you a way to get to and from a job, school, extracurriculars, and any social events you want to go to. You will have to discuss borrowing your parent's car until you can save up to get your own.

Getting involved in your community. Besides making you a more involved member of your community and giving you the chance to give back, being involved lets you meet new people and possibly learn new skills that can benefit you in the future.

Take care of yourself. Eating habits, sleep, and exercise are all part of taking care of yourself, but self-care should also include hygiene and developing good hygiene habits.

Being assertive. Make sure to stand up for yourself in respectful and patient ways. An important part of taking care of yourself is making sure you can stand up for yourself.

Being confident. Belief in yourself is one of the most important things to become self-reliant. You are never truly independent if you must count on other's opinions to make you feel good about yourself.

Staying positive. A sign of maturity is staying upbeat and positive and not letting every little setback or bump in the road get you down. Positivity is important if you want to have a successful and happy life.

DEVELOPING RESPONSIBILITY AND ACCOUNTABILITY

While becoming self-reliant, it's important to show responsibility and accountability. Some ways to make sure you do that include taking charge of your own tasks, taking responsibility for mistakes, being a team player, managing your time, and honoring your commitments.

Taking charge of your tasks means that you don't have to constantly be reminded or asked to do things. Handling your own laundry, washing your dishes, or picking up after yourself are a great place to start. If you must be reminded to take a shower and do your homework, then you aren't being accountable or responsible. Show that you are maturing and learning to handle things on your own by proactively getting these things done.

When you make a mistake, the first step to correcting it is to own your mistake. Openly admit that you made it and find out how to fix it. Lying or avoiding a mistake is something you did as a young child and doesn't reflect the man you are working to become or the accountability you are developing.

Being selfish and expecting the world to revolve around you and your wants is another trait that you are working to outgrow. While it is expected in a younger child, as you get older and develop into a man, it's important to be a team player. This means being considerate toward other people, sharing the rewards, and the recognition.

Managing your time will become more important as you get older. Keep a calendar either on your phone or in a planner to help you remember the dates of practices, tests, games, social events, or job schedules. Keeping track shows that you are responsible enough to participate and accountable enough to do it well.

UNDERSTANDING THE IMPORTANCE OF HARD WORK

No matter what goals you set for yourself or what your plans are, hard work is the key to achieving them. When you work hard and put the effort in, you develop skills and habits that will help you succeed in the future.

Some of the benefits of working hard:

> **Achieving your goals:** If you put in the effort, you are more likely to achieve the goals you've set for yourself. Working hard helps you stay motivated and focused, which makes it more likely that you will achieve what you set out to do.
>
> **Developing skills and habits:** When you are working hard, you don't even realize all the skills you pick up and the good habits you are forming. Hard work is the difference between a person who has productive habits and a person who has toxic habits. You might be developing time management skills, problem-

solving skills, and communication skills without even realizing it.

Being more confident: After working hard and achieving your goals, you will feel so much more confident in yourself and your abilities. This confidence will help you take on new challenges and continue to achieve even greater things.

Being more successful: Success is like dominoes; if you set yourself up correctly, once they begin to fall, they just keep going. Working hard is setting up those first few dominoes and is one of the most important factors in success.

Working hard is not always as easy as it sounds. There will be times when you get tired, feel frustrated, and simply want to give up. However, if it was easy, then it wouldn't be called hard work. Persevere through the challenges, even when they feel like they are never-ending. Remember, when you work hard. You are investing in your future.

PREPARING FOR ADULTHOOD

Preparing for adulthood means that you are developing the skills, knowledge, and attitude that you need to live independently and be responsible for yourself. Building a strong work ethic, having the ability to manage finances, knowing how to make good decisions, and developing and maintaining healthy relationships are all part of that. Everything that you do now will develop your foundation for adulthood and help you decide what kind of life you will have.

CHAPTER THIRTEEN: RESPECTING DIVERSITY AND INCLUSION

Diversity and inclusion are essential to society. In order to have a thriving and peaceful society, you have to learn to embrace the uniqueness of everyone and all of their differences. There are so many ways that someone can be different from you, including their skin color, their religion, the clothes they wear, or their preferred extracurriculars. Focusing on those differences makes it easy to forget that we are all human beings deserving of dignity. If we want to live in a better world, loving the uniqueness of every person and making sure to create an inclusive environment is critical.

Now is the time to start understanding the great things that come with diversity so that you will want to work towards promoting respect, equality, and inclusiveness.

UNDERSTANDING DIFFERENT CULTURES AND BACKGROUNDS

To have respect for diversity, you have to understand how many different cultures there are in the world. Your cultural background is not the only one, and if you keep an open mind, there are so many new things to try and traditions to participate in. Each person has a story unlike anyone else that can be determined by their culture, ethnicity, religion, gender, sexual orientation, and the life experiences that they have had.

Take the time to really learn about different cultures by reading about them. Authors from those countries are the best sources of information, so look for books written by real citizens of those countries. Watching documentaries to try and understand the history and day-to-day life of other people is another way to learn. However, the best way, without a doubt, is to take the time to listen to people. Given the opportunity, people will be happy to share more about their culture and lifestyle. Don't ever assume that you know about a person or a culture until you've taken the time to learn about it. Ignorance is assuming you know more than you do.

Once you take the time to learn about different cultures, it's important to pass that new knowledge and understanding along in the form of educating other people. When you can share the history or experiences of different groups of people, you become part of the solution and not part of the problem. Someone who can't take the time to understand another person's point of view often comes to quick judgments that are wrong.

RECOGNIZING AND COMBATING STEREOTYPES AND PREJUDICES

Stereotypes and prejudices are the building blocks of discrimination, but what exactly are they?

A stereotype is a widely held belief that aims to describe a particular group of people. Most of the time, stereotypes are inaccurate and negative, but even so-called "positive" stereotypes are harmful because they are reductive, limiting, and imposed. They are based on a small group of people and applied to the group at large without consideration for individuals.

Stereotypes come from many different sources. Sometimes, they are based on fear or old social and class structures, animosity between groups (think countries at war, political parties, or even religious groups), language barriers, or economic differences. Other times, they come from propaganda. These usually occur when individuals are represented as oversimplified characteristics of a group. Usually, these beliefs are not based on real facts.

Some ways to avoid stereotyping:

- Never judge an individual based on the group or culture they identify with.
- Actively look for exceptions whenever you hear a new stereotype.
- Question the reason the stereotype was made in the first place. Often, it is linked to an irrational fear and not the actual people belonging to the group.
- Spend time getting to know people different from you.
- Use inclusive language.

Prejudice is a feeling of negativity associated with people based on a fact about them that has been twisted by stereotypes. It's important to be able to recognize these harmful and hurtful behaviors so that you can work against them. Make sure you always question stereotypes and stand up to them and against prejudice any time you encounter it.

In high school, stereotypes tend to be linked to social clicks or groups. Humans generally group together with people who share a common interest. Not understanding other groups or clicks leads to stereotypes forming. These, when left unchecked, can grow into prejudice or the immediate rejection of a person because of the group they belong to, regardless of what the truth is.

Stereotypes are endless, but you shouldn't let them affect the way you see the people in your life. To truly succeed in life, you need to be more than one thing, and you should expect everyone around you to be more than one thing as well. If you are uncertain, get inquisitive and learn more about other people. Knowledge and compassion are the best tools to fight stereotypes and prejudices.

THE IMPORTANCE OF EMPATHY AND UNDERSTANDING

Empathy is the ability to understand how others are feeling and be sympathetic to it. One of the most important parts of empathy is respecting diversity. When you listen to the experiences of other people, you can put yourself in their shoes and imagine what it would feel like.

Being understanding of people different from you allows you to gain more perspective and keep an open mind so that you can start to enjoy people for their uniqueness instead of assuming about them.

ADVOCATING FOR EQUALITY

It should be a fundamental right for people to have equality, but it still isn't possible because of stereotypes, prejudice, systemic oppression, persistent historical hierarchies, and a lack of empathy. Every person needs to actively work to help make the world a better place for everyone rather than a world that judges based on race, gender, sexuality, choice of religion, or disabilities.

Even as a teenager, there are things you can do.

> **Educate yourself so that you are aware of the issue**. If you need to stop and look around, how do you know when there is a problem? Read books, listen to real life stories, and watch documentaries. The more you know about the issues, the more you can stand up against injustice and inequality. If you ever have the time to listen to someone discuss a real-life situation,

make the time to hear it. Your elders can be a wonderful source of first-hand knowledge.

Speak up when you see something you know isn't right. Don't be afraid to speak up against discrimination because the people who don't agree with you aren't people you want to be friends with. The more people that speak up for equality, the more people will have access to it.

Being involved in your community can make a difference as well. Whether you are volunteering for an organization that fights against discrimination, running for office in your school or local organizations, or just making sure you are a positive influence in your local community, every little bit helps.

Use social media to be active while still being respectful and considerate. Consider sharing articles or blogs that talk about issues to help other people become more aware of them. However, you don't want to be part of the problem, which is easy to do if you are getting into fights online. Try to stick to productive, reliable information and avoid personal attacks, misinformation, and extreme language.

Equality is a right, and it is all about celebrating the richness of human diversity. Embrace everyone and not just certain types or groups of people.

While you are standing up for other people, make sure that you stand up for yourself as well. Never let someone tell you that you aren't good enough. Each person deserves equality and a life free from prejudice.

CHAPTER FOURTEEN: OVERCOMING CHALLENGES AND BUILDING RESILIENCE

No one has a perfect life, regardless of what it looks like from the outside. There are challenges that every person must deal with at some point in their life. How you handle these challenges and whether you rise to meet them determine the type of person you are going to be.

UNDERSTANDING FAILURE AND SETBACKS

While no one enjoys failures or setbacks, they are a part of life that you will have to learn to handle. No matter your age, expect to overcome them. It can be especially hard for you because you are still learning so much about yourself and trying to establish yourself.

When you do experience a failure, remember that it is not the end of the world and that everyone you know has faced one at some point or another in their life. Try looking at every failure as a learning experience because you can improve yourself. When you experience a setback, take the time to look at what happened and try to think about what you could have done differently. The point of this is not to beat yourself up but to prepare yourself for future situations.

If you spend the time to reflect on what you would have liked to have done differently, the next time a similar situation arises, you'll be better prepared for it. Don't focus on the negative of what happened; instead, you should focus on the positives of future opportunities.

Some failures you might face include:

> **Academic Setbacks:** You might have been working to pull your math grade up but still received a bad grade on the last test. While this will delay you getting your grade up, it doesn't mean you still can't do it. You should spend some time figuring out what went wrong. Did you not spend enough time studying? Maybe

you don't understand the material and need a tutor? You can address the root cause of why you failed before your next test.

Athletic Setbacks: Maybe you didn't make a team that you really wanted to. There is always next season that you can try out again, but you need to determine why you didn't make the team. Try going to talk to the coach and just ask what they would like to see from you so that you know what to practice. Work on your own to hone your skills, or look for other people who are good enough to help you improve. Don't let negative feelings make you feel like you can't do it, as disappointment or frustration aren't helpful emotions.

Social Setbacks: Sometimes, you can have disappointments in your social life, such as when you plan a party or event but are met with a poor turnout. Instead of worrying about the people who didn't show up, focus on the ones who did show up and plan to have a different type of event next time. Maybe you didn't get invited to an event that you were wanting to be included in. Don't let that hurt your feelings. Focus on building new social connections and branching out. The more people you get out and meet, the more friendships you'll be likely to develop.

Personal Setbacks: A lot of times, when you set goals, it doesn't mean you are going to hit them right away. Maybe you set a goal to get in better shape or eat healthy, and you've had to start and stop a few times. Don't let that dissuade you from looking for ways to move forward. Figure out why you have gotten off track and create a new plan that addresses the reasons you've struggled. If you are having trouble with your goals, try finding a friend who has some of the same goals, so you'll have a buddy to work with.

Failures aren't a reason to get yourself down. Instead, use them as a chance to learn from mistakes and do better next time.

STRATEGIES FOR BUILDING RESILIENCE

When you experience a failure or a setback, you have another opportunity to meet your goal next time. The opportunity to build resilience, which is the ability to recover from setbacks.

It's such an important skill to have, and it will be especially helpful for you because the world can be a tough place with unavoidable setbacks that you'll need to overcome. If you are resilient, you'll be able to keep going and pick yourself up.

There are some simple ways to develop resilience.

> **Learn from your mistakes.** Take that time to learn what went wrong and what you could have done differently. When you make changes so that you can succeed, you'll be more resilient for it.
>
> **Don't give up, and don't let negative feelings overwhelm you.** When things get tough, the easiest thing to do is give up, but resilience will help you keep going. A key difference between successful and unsuccessful people is the amount of resilience they possess.
>
> **Talk to someone you trust about how you are struggling if you feel like you can't overcome your setbacks.** A trusted adult can help you see different options that you might not have thought about originally. Having a strong support system can make all the difference for teens or adults. This support can make any situation easier to handle.

Learning how to bounce back from failure is a skill that will help you in all areas of your life. Learning not to sweat the small stuff is a healthy mentality to have, as opposed to constantly stressing over and internalizing everything.

When you are not afraid of failing, you are more likely to try new things and achieve new accomplishments, which leads to new opportunities. One step to being resilient is to be an optimist and not a pessimist.

An optimist is someone who expects good outcomes and avoids problems by being resilient and moving past failures. Optimistic people tend to have better coping skills, better health, and lower stress levels.

A pessimist is someone who expects the worst from every situation. They tend to embody a "gloom and doom" attitude. Oftentimes, when you expect the worst, you will get the worst.

THE ROLE OF A POSITIVE MINDSET

Your teenage years can be a time of change and challenges, and it's easy to get overwhelmed and feel defeated. Maintaining a positive mindset will keep you from falling into a downward spiral. A positive mindset helps keep sad thoughts and negative feelings from pulling you away from the person you want to be and the goals you want to achieve.

A positive mindset is a mental attitude that leads you to focus on the good part of any situation. It's part of seeing opportunities instead of failures and keeping your chin up even when a situation is hard.

Cultivating a positive mindset helps you keep focused on the good things in life. Although it's not always possible to make sure every thought is a happy one, there are ways to counteract those negative thoughts when they come up. One way to do this is through gratitude. Even if you can't come up with anything deeper than gratitude for electricity or your cell phone, the act itself becomes a practice that can shift your mindset in the right direction. When you feel yourself getting stuck, start listing off everything that you appreciate about your life and your current circumstances. The more often you practice this, the more aware you'll become of the good around you.

Since it's much more enjoyable to be around people with upbeat attitudes, spending time with genuinely positive individuals may make you feel better. This will then allow you to have that same effect on the people around you. No one wants to hang out with a gloomy person that makes them feel worse all the time.

LEARNING FROM MISTAKES AND EXPERIENCES

As a teenager, you are going to make mistakes as you grow. Everyone did. While you are trying new things, making new friends, and learning new things, keep in mind that mistakes are not the focus; the experiences you get from them are the most important.

Remember:

- Don't be scared to own up to your mistakes.
- Look back so that you can understand your mistakes. This is the only way to avoid them in the future.
- Don't get bogged down worrying about past mistakes. Once you move on, stay there.
- Ask for help when you need it because everyone needs a little help.

The best way to get experience is to make mistakes, so focus on looking at mistakes as a chance to learn and grow. This is a lifelong process because you'll never stop making mistakes. You just need to learn to love and embrace them so that you make fewer and fewer over time.

CONCLUSION: STEPPING INTO ADULTHOOD

While you are embarking on this exciting time of your life, you'll discover that it is the gateway to so many amazing things. No two men have walked the exact same path but remember that you are not alone. Every man has walked this path in his own way.

There will be challenges and triumphs along the way, and maybe this survival guide has given you some of the tools you need to survive the next few years. No matter how much of a struggle it might be during these teen years, don't forget you have an entire life ahead of you. Focus on setting yourself up for an awesome life.

Take a moment to reflect and look back at whether you feel any more prepared now than you did before and if you are the same person who started reading this book. Did you learn anything?

Embrace changes as they come and realize you have so much incredible potential inside of you. Puberty is all about self-exploration and self-discovery. Make sure to get out there and try new things, make those mistakes, and learn from them so you can continue traveling down the sometimes-rocky path to your full potential.

Make sure you set your goals high and believe in your ability to achieve anything you set your mind to if you are willing to put in the hard work. Perseverance, hard work, and education can take you anywhere you want to go, especially if you surround yourself with positive people and keep a positive attitude yourself.

Since life is a journey, think of your teenage years as the first leg of the journey, not the end of it. This is more of the planning stage to decide what kind of journey you'll have and where you will go while on it.

Make sure to treat other people with kindness, empathy, and compassion while using your voice to stand up for yourself and others. Live in a way that positively impacts others. You have the power to shape the future into something remarkable and amazing, so go do it.

Printed in Great Britain
by Amazon